Black Americans of Achievement

LEGACY EDITION

Langston Hughes

POET

Black Americans of Achievement

L E G A C Y   E D I T I O N

Langston Hughes

POET

Jack Rummel

With additional text written by
Heather Lehr Wagner

Consulting Editor, Revised Edition
Heather Lehr Wagner

Senior Consulting Editor, First Edition
Nathan Irvin Huggins
Director, W.E.B. Du Bois Institute
for Afro-American Research
Harvard University

CHELSEA HOUSE
P U B L I S H E R S
An imprint of Infobase Publishing

COVER: Poet and writer Langston Hughes photographed on a Harlem street in 1958.

Langston Hughes

Copyright © 2005 by Infobase Publishing

Chelsea House
An imprint of Infobase Publishing
132 West 31st Street
New York, NY 10001

ISBN-10: 0-7910-8250-4
ISBN-13: 978-0-7910-8250-8

Library of Congress Cataloging-in-Publication Data

Rummel, Jack.
  Langston Hughes/Jack Rummel; with additional text by Heather Lehr Wagner.
    p. cm.—(Black Americans of achievement)
    ISBN 0-7910-8250-4 (hardcover)
  1. Hughes, Langston, 1902–1967—Juvenile literature. 2. Poets, American—20th century—Biography—Juvenile literature. 3. African American poets—Biography—Juvenile literature. [1. Hughes, Langston, 1902–1967.] I. Wagner, Heather Lehr. II. Title. III. Series.
  PS3515.U274Z7754 2005
  818'.5209—dc22   2004019397

Series and cover design by Keith Trego

Printed in the United States of America

Bang 21C 10 9 8 7 6 5 4 3 2

This book is printed on acid-free paper.

Contents

Introduction

Nearly 20 years ago, Chelsea House Publishers began to publish the first volumes in the series called BLACK AMERICANS OF ACHIEVEMENT. This series eventually numbered over a hundred books and profiled outstanding African Americans from many walks of life. Today, if you ask school teachers and school librarians what comes to mind when you mention Chelsea House, many will say—"Black Americans of Achievement."

The mix of individuals whose lives we covered was eclectic, to say the least. Some were well known—Muhammad Ali and Dr. Martin Luther King, Jr, for example. But others, such as Harriet Tubman and Sojourner Truth, were lesser-known figures who were introduced to modern readers through these books. The individuals profiled were chosen for their actions, their deeds, and ultimately their influence on the lives of others and their impact on our nation as a whole. By sharing these stories of unique Americans, we hoped to illustrate how ordinary individuals can be transformed by extraordinary circumstances to become people of greatness. We also hoped that these special stories would encourage young-adult readers to make their own contribution to a better world. Judging from the many wonderful letters we have received about the BLACK AMERICANS OF ACHIEVEMENT biographies over the years from students, librarians, and teachers, they have certainly fulfilled the goal of inspiring others!

Now, some 20 years later, we are publishing 18 volumes of the original BLACK AMERICANS OF ACHIEVEMENT series in revised editions to bring the books into the twenty-first century and make them available to a new generation of young-adult readers. The selection was based on the importance of these figures to American life and the popularity of the original books with our readers. These revised editions have a new full-color design and, wherever possible, we have added color photographs. The books have new features, including quotes from the writings and speeches of leaders and interesting and unusual facts about their lives. The concluding section of each book gives new emphasis to the legacy of these men and women for the current generation of readers.

The lives of these African-American leaders are unique and remarkable. By transcending the barriers that racism placed in their paths, they are examples of the power and resiliency of the human spirit and are an inspiration to readers.

We present these wonderful books to our audience for their reading pleasure.

Lee M. Marcott
Chelsea House Publishers
August 2004

1

At the Crossroads

Glinting in the last rays of sunset, the train slows as it approaches East St. Louis, Missouri. As the staccato, tapping sounds of the train wheels change to a steadier beat, a young man sitting at the window of the train watches the small dramas of town life in 1920 unfold before him: a chocolate-colored man, hands in pockets, trudges home at the end of a long day's work in a factory; children in brightly colored clothes shout excitedly as they play a ball game in a rutted street; two women sit on the stoop of their apartment building, talking quietly.

Soon the train is at the edge of the city and begins to climb onto a river bridge. As the young man stares out the window at the choppy waters of the huge Mississippi River, he thinks about how the flow of his own life links him to the people he has just been watching. He pulls an envelope from his pocket and picks up his pen, and on the envelope he begins writing a poem that he calls "The Negro Speaks of Rivers":

I've known rivers:
I've known rivers ancient as the world and older
    than the flow of human blood in human veins.
My soul has grown deep like the rivers.

I bathed in the Euphrates when dawns were young.
I built my hut near the Congo and it lulled me to sleep.
I looked upon the Nile and raised the pyramids above it.
I heard the singing of the Mississippi when Abe
    Lincoln went down to New Orleans, and I've seen
    its muddy bosom turn all golden in the sunset.

I've known rivers:
Ancient, dusky rivers.

My soul has grown deep like the rivers.

Langston Hughes wrote this now-celebrated poem during the summer of 1920, at a time when he was approaching a crossroads in his life. Having just graduated from high school at the age of 18, he understood that his adolescence was quickly drawing to a close and that the time was coming for him to make his way in the world. Yet he felt as though there was no one he could count on for support or advice.

Just as Langston was traveling alone on a train across America, so had he been forced to go through most of his life on his own. Shortly before he was born, his father left his mother and went abroad. His mother then left Langston to be raised by his grandmother and family friends while she searched for work. She returned to take care of Langston only when an opportunity allowed her to stay with him.

Langston got to know his father even less well than he knew his mother. He and his father first met in 1907, when Langston was five years old and his family was briefly reunited in Mexico. He and his father next met 12 years later,

Langston Hughes in a 1920 photograph. Hughes published his first poem at 19 and went on to become one of the leading voices in the artistic movement known as the Harlem Renaissance.

when Langston's father, who was traveling from New York City to his home in Toluca, Mexico, wrote to his 17-year-old son, who was living in Cleveland, Ohio: "You are to accompany me to Mexico for the summer." This surprising summons pleased Langston, who immediately looked forward to spending time with a father whom he did not know well but about whom he had many illusions. He dreamed that his father, who had become a successful businessman, was "a kind of strong, bronze cowboy, in a big Mexican hat, going back and forth from his business in the city to his ranch in the mountains."

Yet Langston's vacation in Mexico that summer did not turn out to be a pleasant one. His father proved to be cold and disagreeable rather than kind and wonderful. Racing from one business appointment to another, he paid little attention to his son except to insist that he take up accounting, a subject for which Langston had neither the aptitude nor the desire. Langston felt so overwhelmed by his father's cold-heartedness and badgering that he wrote to his mother, "I began to wish I had never been born—not under such circumstances."

When the following summer arrived, however, Langston felt that he had little choice but to turn once more to his father. Having just completed high school, Langston realized that if he was to get ahead in the world, he would need help from someone—and his father was the only person he knew who had enough money to offer that help. Langston's mother, who had returned to Cleveland to live with Langston while he was still in high school, was insisting that he remain with her after his graduation. Her second marriage had failed, and by staying in Cleveland, Langston could help support her and her stepson, Gwyn.

Langston had his own plans for his future, however, so he was not anxious to fulfill his mother's wishes even though he sympathized with them. He realized that what she wanted would mean the end of his schooling. Furthermore, it would mean the end of his chance to experience the larger world beyond the Midwest, where he had grown up.

Having spent most of his childhood without anyone taking very much interest in him, Langston was now unwilling to sacrifice his freedom for any member of his family. He had dreams of his own. He had decided that he was going to become a poet.

Hughes had been elected class poet when he was in the eighth grade, and at the graduation ceremonies at the end of the school year he had recited a poem he had written for his classmates and fellow students. The enthusiastic applause that followed his reading had made a huge impression on him. "That was the way I began to write poetry," he said. Having received little attention or encouragement while he was growing up, he enjoyed hearing the audience's approval and realized that if he continued to write poems, he could receive additional praise.

Possessing the single-mindedness that any artist must have if he wants to be a success, Langston became determined to strike out on his own and devote himself completely to his education and his art. His plan for accomplishing this was a bold one. It consisted of convincing his father to pay for his college costs at Columbia University in New York City, where Langston wished to continue his studies. A college education from such a prestigious institution would go a long way toward ensuring his success as a well-respected poet.

SEEKING SUPPORT

As Langston journeyed from Cleveland to St. Louis in 1920 and headed toward another reunion with his father in Mexico, he tried to remain hopeful that his father would agree to spend the money. Because his father had not been around to help him in the past, Langston reasoned, he might be interested in helping him prepare for the future. Despite having an unkind nature, his father had shown himself to be a very practical-minded man.

Langston's father did not think that his son's plans were very practical at all. Shortly after Langston arrived in Mexico, his father told him that he would not be sent to Columbia in the fall. For a black man to pursue a career as a poet was foolish, according to his father. He could never manage to make a living as a writer.

Langston's father proposed an alternative plan. First, Langston would work for a year in Mexico. He would then go to college abroad, in Switzerland or Germany, to study mining engineering. Once Langston's studies were completed, he would return to work in Mexico—and not in the United States. His father explained that because Langston was black, he would not have a chance to amount to anything in America. In Mexico, where racial prejudice was not nearly as strong as it was in the United States, he could live a good life and become rich.

Langston refused to be manipulated so easily by his father and rejected the future his parent had mapped out for him. He promptly found work in Toluca, teaching English in a private school in the morning and giving lessons at a business college in the afternoon. These jobs not only freed him from his dependence on his father, but also enabled him to begin saving a bit of money—not, however, nearly enough to enroll in Columbia later that summer.

Instead of sending himself to New York in September, Langston decided to send three poems he had written during the summer to *The Brownies' Book*, a newly established magazine for black children, whose offices were located in New York City. Jessie Fauset, the editor of the magazine, replied to Langston in early October that she wanted to publish one of them, making it the first of his poems to achieve widespread publication. Fauset also asked him to send her other poems and stories he had written.

Within a few months, Langston saw several of his poems, a short play, an essay, and some short stories published in *The Brownies' Book*, as well as in *The Crisis*, a companion magazine aimed at a black-adult audience. Published by the National Association for the Advancement of Colored People (NAACP), *The Crisis* was edited by Fauset and W.E.B. Du Bois, an influential educator and author who headed a small but growing group of black artists and intellectuals based in Harlem, New York. These men and women were in the process of creating a revolution in black art, thought, and music that came to be known as the "Harlem Renaissance." Langston felt determined to become a member of this select group in Harlem when *The Crisis* accepted "The Negro Speaks of Rivers" in January 1921. Before he could establish himself as a figure in New York's literary scene, however, he first had to arrive there.

Langston was still based in Mexico half a year later, when the summer of 1921 arrived, yet the time he spent outside the United States proved to be of longstanding value to him. Having learned to speak Spanish, he traveled to Mexico City on weekends to see bullfights and to visit friends. He also encountered a new kind of art, which included the paintings of Diego Rivera and David Siquieros and the writings of Carlos Pellicer. This art did not make use of traditional European images and themes, as most contemporary art did. Instead, these Mexican artists examined their own culture in their art. From these artists, Langston learned to look at his own race when he was in search of material about which to write.

Seeing that his son's works were being published on a regular basis by *The Crisis*, Langston's father eventually became so impressed by his son's accomplishments that he could not deny his demands. Langston's father offered to pay the costs for his son's first year in New York if he promised to study engineering at Columbia. Langston agreed to this offer, applied for admission to the school, and was accepted at once.

In late August 1921 Langston boarded a steamship bound for New York from Veracruz, Mexico, a port city on the Gulf of Mexico. Veracruz was hot and humid at that time of the year, and the uncomfortable climate made Langston all the more eager to leave Mexico for New York. As the ship slipped

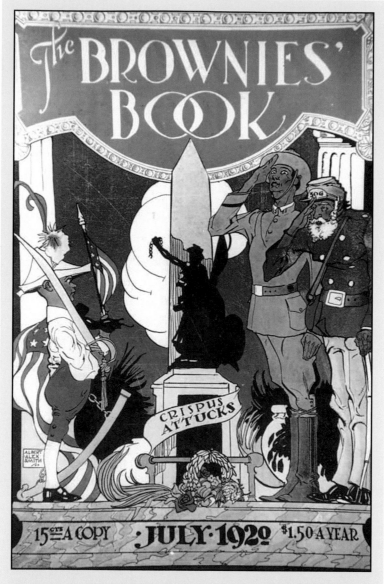

The Brownies' Book, a magazine geared toward black children, was the first major publication to accept one of Hughes's poems. Within a few months, Hughes had published several more works in *The Brownies' Book*, as well as *The Crisis*, the magazine of the National Association for the Advancement of Colored People (NAACP).

out of the harbor and into the foggy gulf, he could do little but think about the city of New York that awaited him. Another black writer, James Weldon Johnson, had claimed that New York was soon going to be "the greatest Negro city in the world," and Langston looked forward to contributing to that greatness.

2

A Lonely Youth

James Langston Hughes was born on February 1, 1902, in Joplin, Missouri. He was named James, after his father, but this name was eventually dropped and he became known as Langston. The only child of James and Carrie Hughes, he never knew what it was like to belong to a happy, closely knit family.

James and Carrie Hughes had been unhappy with one another from the beginning of their marriage, and the reasons for their unhappiness had as much to do with the color of their skin and the society into which they had been born as they did with their contrasting personalities. Like most blacks who grew up in nineteenth-century America, they were victims of white attitudes and discriminatory laws. In James Hughes's case, being subjected to racial prejudice did not make him feel bitter toward whites so much as it caused him to develop a great deal of contempt for most members of his own race.

The feeling of contempt increased after James Hughes and his wife moved to Oklahoma from Kentucky in the late 1890s. A well-educated man, Hughes taught school in Oklahoma while he studied for the bar exam. His plans for the future were to practice law and buy land. These hopes were soon dashed when the state of Oklahoma barred blacks from taking the exam.

Although James Hughes was angry at white society for denying him a chance to pursue his chosen profession as well as his basic civil rights, he chose to blame his own race even more for these injustices. He believed that rather than being the victims of oppression, blacks lacked ambition and therefore were responsible for their status as second-class citizens. This kind of spiteful thinking made James Hughes a hard and bitter man. He seemed to feel hatred for everyone, including himself.

In temperament, the young Langston proved to be the opposite of his father. Whereas his father was bitter, Langston was easygoing and understanding, especially when it came to his feelings toward other blacks. Yet his courteous and gentle-hearted nature could not prevent him from falling victim to a lonely childhood.

After Langston's parents were separated, his mother left him for long periods of time while she moved from city to city in search of work. During these periods he lived mostly in Lawrence, Kansas, with his grandmother, Mary Langston, who was about 70 years old when Langston first started to live with her. She was a strong-willed woman who was fiercely opposed to racial discrimination, and she tried to protect her grandson from discrimination of any kind. Accordingly, Langston learned from her to fight racial prejudice, but he also lived a sheltered life when he was under her care.

While Langston was growing up, he also stayed occasionally in Lawrence at the home of some family friends, James ("Uncle") and Mary ("Auntie") Reed. "For me," Langston said, "there have never been any better people in the world. I loved them very much." Although the Reeds, like his grandmother, treated him well, their kindness could not make up for a lack of affection from his parents. Living with his grandmother and the Reeds in all-white neighborhoods, Langston often felt even more isolated. As he grew older, several experiences away from his home compounded his feeling of loneliness.

When Langston was ready to start going to school in 1908, his mother was told that because her son was black, he could not attend a nearby, chiefly white school in Topeka, Kansas. He would have to go to a school for black children across town. Langston's mother fought with the school board over this decision. Since she worked every day, she argued, she was unable to bring Langston to a school that was so far away and he was too young to travel through the streets of the city by himself. Carrie Hughes won her argument, and Langston was allowed to enter the first grade of the nearby school.

Once in school, Langston was made to sit in a far corner of the classroom, at the end of the last row. He came to feel so isolated in school that his mother removed him from class before the year had ended.

When a similar situation occurred six years later, Langston had grown old and bold enough under his grandmother's guidance to fight back. After he and his black classmates were moved into a separate row, away from the white children, he wrote up signs that said "Jim Crow Row" (a reference to then legally permissible discriminatory practices against blacks known as Jim Crow laws). He gave a sign to each black student to put on his or her desk. This led to Langston's being expelled from the school. A protest from a group of parents over the teacher's discrimination got Langston reinstated, and separate seating for blacks and whites was no longer allowed.

Fortunately, neither of these experiences affected Langston's desire to learn. Throughout his life, he remained an exceptionally eager and able student, excelling wherever he studied.

Langston's sense of isolation increased when he was 12 years old. He was taken to church by Auntie Reed to experience the

After his parents separated, Hughes (foreground) grew up in Lawrence, Kansas, with his grandmother. During this time Hughes often felt lost and lonely, and he began writing stories and poetry to deal with his feelings.

feeling of being "saved" by Jesus. As the church service progressed, the members of the congregation came forward one by one and announced that Jesus had entered their hearts. Gradually, all the members of the congregation except Langston came forward to say that they had been saved.

Langston had not felt anything, and he did not want to pretend that he had. Yet the congregation waited for him to come forward, and Auntie Reed prayed for him. To escape from the unbearable pressure that he felt was being placed upon him, Langston announced at last that he, too, had been saved. His pronouncement made the congregation shout with joy.

Later that night, after everyone in Auntie Reed's house had gone to bed, Langston broke down and cried. He said:

> That night, for the last time in my life but one—for I was a big boy of twelve years old—I cried, in bed alone, and couldn't stop. I buried my head under the quilts, but my aunt heard me. She woke up and told my uncle I was crying because the Holy Ghost had come into my life, and because I had seen Jesus. But I was really crying because I couldn't bear to tell her that I had lied, and I had deceived everybody in the church, that I hadn't seen Jesus, and that now I didn't believe there was a Jesus any more, since he didn't come to help me.

ESCAPING REALITY

One of the ways that Langston sought to overcome his loneliness was by losing himself in a private world of stories. His grandmother, wearing her first husband's bullet-riddled shawl (which had been in his possession when he was killed in John Brown's raid on Harper's Ferry just before the start of the Civil War), recounted to Langston how his forebears had fought against slavery. "She sat, looking very much like an Indian in her rocker," he said, "and read the Bible or held me in her lap and told me long beautiful stories about people who wanted to make Negroes free."

Another way in which he attempted to deal with his feelings of loneliness was by writing poetry. Writing enabled him to let out his feelings and express what he felt, by forcing him to take a searching look at himself and the world around him.

Langston's love for the written word prompted him to become a frequent visitor to the library in Lawrence. The atmosphere of the library held a certain mystique for him. "The silence . . . the big chairs, and long tables, and the fact that the library was always there and didn't have . . . any sort of insecurity about it—all made me love it," Langston said. "I believed in books more than people."

Langston also loved the theater, along with what was then the newest invention in American culture, the motion picture. His mother, who had wanted to be an actress, took him to the theater when he visited her in Kansas City, and the theater came to hold the same attraction for him that it did for her. Although Langston enjoyed movies, the Lawrence movie theaters' policy of racially segregated seating outraged his grandmother. She forbade him to see movies, and Langston complied with her wishes.

When Langston's grandmother died in 1915, he went to live with his mother; her second husband, Homer Clark; and Clark's two-year-old son, Gwyn. Langston's new family moved to wherever Clark could find work. They went from Lawrence, Kansas, to Kansas City, Missouri, to Lincoln, Illinois. With every move, it seemed more and more as though Langston did not have a true home—until his family arrived in Cleveland, Ohio, in the summer of 1916. Langston enrolled in Cleveland's Central High School and attended classes there for four years.

Soon after the family moved to Cleveland, Clark began to feel that his marriage to Carrie was failing, and he left abruptly for Chicago, Illinois. Langston's mother took Gwyn and followed her husband to Chicago, hoping for a reconciliation. Fifteen-year-old Langston was left behind in Cleveland, forced to care for himself in an attic room that he rented in someone's house. "I couldn't afford to eat in a restaurant, and the only thing which I knew how to cook myself in the kitchen where I roomed was rice. . . . Then I read myself to sleep," he said. His mother and Gwyn did not return to Cleveland to live with him until nearly two years later, in the spring of 1919.

EDUCATION IN CLEVELAND

To make up for his unstable home life, Langston devoted himself to his classwork and to other interests as well. He participated in a number of extracurricular activities while he attended Central High. Besides joining the editorial staff of the school magazine, known as the *Monthly*, he was elected to the student council, he was a standout member of the school's track team, he was an officer in the drill corps, and he acted in school plays.

Central High proved to be a good place for Langston to go to school. One of the oldest and most distinguished secondary schools in Cleveland, it had traditionally been the school where Cleveland's white elite—including John D. Rockefeller, the great financier and philanthropist—had been educated. By the time Langston arrived at Central High, its student body was more ethnically diverse than it had been in the past.

Waves of immigrants had recently hit the Northern industrial states as people came looking for work from Eastern and Southern Europe as well as from the Southern United States. Because very little industry was taking place in Europe while World War I was being fought there, the industrial North sought to increase its productivity. Cities such as Cleveland attracted people from all over the globe.

Langston's best friend in high school was Satur Andrzejewski, a young man whose family had emigrated from Poland. Several of Langston's other friends, who worked with him on the *Monthly*, were from Jewish families that had come from Eastern Europe and Russia. Langston's Jewish friends at Central High made an especially lasting impression on him, for they were the ones who first introduced him to the ideas of socialism.

Socialism is the doctrine that all property in a society is public property. This property is then divided among the people in the society so that all men and women share equally in the fruits of each other's labors. This concept appealed to Langston partly because he did not have very much he could call his own and partly because he wanted every man and woman to be treated fairly and equally. He began to read socialist magazines such as the *Socialist Call* and the *Liberator*, as well as books by authors with politically radical points of view, such as John Reed's *Ten Days That Shook the World*, which describes the Russian Revolution in 1917. Claude McKay, a black writer whose articles and poems appeared in the *Liberator*, became a particular favorite of Langston's.

While Langston was reading these authors, he had reason to believe that he, too, had a talent for writing. During his four years at Central High, he wrote a number of poems and short

DID YOU KNOW?

It was while Hughes was a student at Cleveland's Central High that friends first introduced him to the tenets of socialism. In socialism, Hughes found a political system that he felt was committed to principles of equality. Later, as an adult, he traveled to Russia and found in the Communist system that governed the country an ideology that he believed was successfully stamping out racism and poverty.

Hughes's outspoken support for the principles of socialism and communism would prove costly, both personally and professionally. On March 26, 1953, Hughes was called before the McCarthy committee, a group within the U.S. House of Representatives investigating what it labeled "un-American activities." Hughes' pro-Communist sympathies were well known and documented in his writings, and his appearance before the committee caused some professional readings and appearances to be cancelled.

Hughes was relatively fortunate that he was eventually able to continue with his career. Other artists "blacklisted" by their association with the American Communist Party were forced to leave the country or could no longer find work.

stories for the *Monthly*. Many of his early poems reveal an unpolished beginner searching to find his poetic voice, but Langston gradually began to understand what kind of poetry he wanted to write. He composed a number of poems about social injustice that made use of free verse rather than a traditional verse form such as the sonnet. These poems show the influence of the favorite poets of Langston's youth, Carl Sandburg and Walt Whitman.

In other poems, Langston began to employ Negro dialects as well as the words and rhythms of the music he had heard when he was taken to black churches and Sunday school by Auntie Reed. In still others he sought to capture either street talk or the music known as the blues. The mournful, lonely sound of the blues held a special appeal for Langston.

An example of Langston's evolving style can be seen in a poem that he wrote to a high school sweetheart, a young black girl who had recently moved to Cleveland from the South. The poem is called "When Sue Wears Red."

When Susanna Jones wears red
Her face is like an ancient cameo
Turned brown by the ages.

Come with a blast of trumpets,
Jesus!

When Susanna Jones wears red
A queen from some time-dead Egyptian night
Walks once again.
Blow trumpets, Jesus!
And the beauty of Susanna Jones in red
Wakes in my heart a love-fire sharp like a pain.

Sweet silver trumpets,
Jesus!

In this poem, Langston compares Sue's beauty with the classic beauty of an ancient cameo and an African queen and echoes his comparisons with the delighted, religious cries of "Jesus!" Combining images from ancient and modern times, the poem is a celebration of all black beauty.

Most of Langston's early poems focused on how it felt and what it meant to be black. Because several members of his family—particularly his grandmother—had a history of championing black rights, Langston was well acquainted with the problems that confronted blacks. He often felt a bit removed from other blacks while he was growing up because he lived in all-white neighborhoods and went to mostly white schools. The sounds and music of black culture attracted him, however. Above all, he could identify with black culture's theme of feeling alienated from the rest of society. Having no specific family to whom he could feel close, he ultimately sought to embrace all of black society in his poetry.

Langston's strategy of capturing black sights and black sounds would serve him particularly well in the days to come, when he would settle in the mostly black community of Harlem, New York.

3

The Harlem Renaissance

Langston Hughes arrived in New York City by steamship on the evening of September 4, 1921. The city's famous skyline dazzled the 19 year old. "There is no thrill in all the world," he said, "like entering, for the first time, New York harbor—coming in from the flat monotony of the sea to this rise of dreams and beauty. New York is truly the dream city." After helping some of his fellow passengers find their way around New York, he took a subway uptown, to 135th Street in Harlem, and rented a room at the Harlem YMCA.

Harlem in the 1920s was the largest and most influential black community in the United States. Not only was it a center of black intellectual life, but it was an artistic center as well. Hughes ached to plunge headlong into this stimulating neighborhood, but he had an obligation to fulfill: he had to attend Columbia University. Accordingly, after staying for a few days at the Harlem YMCA, he paid a visit to the Columbia housing office to secure a dormitory room for himself.

During the time that Hughes was entering college, most universities made it very hard for blacks to gain admission. The few blacks who were admitted to such universities usually had to live in segregated dormitories or else find private housing off campus. In this respect, Columbia University was no different than other universities. Hughes had difficulty in getting a dormitory room even though he had applied for and had been granted one in advance. He finally talked a housing officer into letting him have a room on campus, and he became the only black student during that year to live in a university dormitory.

He enrolled in a standard course of freshman studies: English, French, contemporary civilization, physical education, and physics. His classes, however, did not interest him (the mathematics taught in the physics course that his father insisted he take was completely beyond him). He preferred to indulge himself in his love for the theater.

During Hughes's first year in New York, he attended the hit Broadway musical of the season, Eubie Blake and Noble Sissle's *Shuffle Along*. The play featured the singer Florence Mills and—for one of the first times on a Broadway stage—an all-black cast. He also saw Eugene O'Neill's *The Hairy Ape* and *Anna Christie*, George Bernard Shaw's *Mrs. Warren's Profession*, a production by a theater group from Moscow, and a number of other plays.

Several months into the fall semester, Hughes received a letter from Jessie Fauset, his editor at *The Brownies' Book* and *The Crisis*. He had been so shy about meeting the well-known editors of *The Crisis* that he had not yet told them that he had moved to New York. Once Fauset found out that he was in town, she invited him to meet her and W.E.B. Du Bois at the offices of the NAACP (Du Bois had co-founded the National

Negro Committee, which later became the NAACP). Hughes accepted her invitation. Accompanied by his mother, who had come to see him in New York, he met Fauset, Du Bois, and other members of the *Crisis* and NAACP staffs. This was an important meeting for Hughes; it was his initial introduction into a circle of people who would influence black thought in twentieth-century America.

Fauset was impressed enough with Hughes to offer him a standing invitation to visit her home in Harlem. Others who attended this meeting were equally impressed. Augustus Granville Dill, the business manager of *The Crisis*, invited Hughes to spend his Christmas vacation at Dill's apartment. Accompanied by Dill and other *Crisis* workers, Hughes subsequently attended concerts and lectures, and he dined at the few private clubs in New York that were open to black membership.

While leading a full cultural life in New York, Hughes managed to achieve good grades at Columbia. At the end of the first semester he had a B-plus average. He was becoming more and more dissatisfied with his life as a student at a prestigious Ivy League school, however. White students kept him at a cool distance; his only real school friend was a Chinese student from Honolulu. Hughes wanted to write for the school newspaper, the *Spectator*, but the only assignment that was given to him was to write a column covering the white fraternities. Because he was black and no one in the fraternities would talk to him, it was an impossible assignment to fulfill.

Langston's father was grudgingly sending his son money to pay for that first year in New York, as he had promised he would, but he demanded to know how Langston spent the money and how he was doing in school. When he found out that Langston had not made A's in all of his subjects, he threatened to stop sending money. Eventually he relented, and Langston received $300—enough to pay for an overcoat and expenses to last through the winter.

Jessie Fauset, editor of *The Brownies' Book* and *The Crisis*, welcomed Hughes to New York and introduced him to influential Harlem blacks, who were all impressed with the young poet. Fauset mentored Hughes and helped him reach a larger audience with his poetry.

In May 1922, Hughes received word that his father had suffered a stroke and was critically ill. By this time Hughes had made up his mind to spend more time on his poetry and to leave Columbia. He also wanted to spend more time in Harlem. There, he said, "Everybody seemed to make me welcome," which was not how he was treated at Columbia.

Hughes wrote to his father to inform him of this decision and to return the latest check that had come to him from Mexico. When he received no reply after a month, he wrote another letter, then another. He finally received a reply from his father's housekeeper that his father's health was improving and then stopped writing to him altogether.

After finishing the spring term, Hughes moved to Harlem and tried to find a job. He answered ad after ad in the newspapers, only to be told by his would-be employers that they were looking for whites only. At last he found a job as a laborer on a vegetable farm outside the city. It was hard work, and it did not leave him any time to write, but Hughes was content to have a break from mental labor for a while.

By early September, the growing season was over and the workers were let go. Hughes next worked for a florist, but then, tired of low-paying, city-bound jobs, he searched along the docks of New York for work aboard a ship. He landed a job on a freighter called the *Oronoke*, but much to his surprise, the ship was not bound for foreign lands. Instead, it headed up the Hudson River to be put into storage at Jones Point, New York, along with dozens of other freighters that were no longer needed after the end of the World War I.

Despite Hughes's tremendous disappointment at not getting a chance to sail abroad, he decided to stay in upstate New York with the crew that watched over the ships. His life at Jones Point was quiet. The work was light, there was plenty of time to write, and he was regularly given leave, during which time he visited New York and Washington, D.C. He also spent some of his leave with his friend Countee Cullen in Harlem.

Hughes had spent a lot of his time during his first year in New York at the Harlem branch of the New York Public Library. One of the persons he met there was Cullen, an up-and-coming poet. The two men got along well and traded poems with one another for appraisal and criticism.

Cullen and Hughes approached their poetry in different ways. Cullen was interested in poetry that demanded exact syllable counts and certain sounds to complete a rhyme scheme. Hughes, on the other hand, preferred to write in free verse.

Countee Cullen

One of Hughes' friends and rivals during the Harlem Renaissance was poet Countee Cullen. Cullen was born on May 30, 1903. Originally named Countee Porter, he was adopted by a Methodist minister and his wife, Reverend and Mrs. Frederick Cullen.

Cullen wrote poetry throughout his school years. While he was attending New York University, his poetry began to be published in W.E.B. Du Bois' *The Crisis* and the National Urban League's publication, *Opportunity*. Cullen later became the assistant editor for *Opportunity*. His first book of poetry, *Color*, was published in 1923—the same year that he graduated from college. Cullen went on to attend Harvard University, where he earned a master's degree in English and French.

In 1927, Cullen's second volume of poetry, *Copper Sun*, was published. This collection was received more critically in the black community because its poetry contained less of a focus on racial issues than that of *Color*. Unlike Hughes, Cullen chose to focus less on racial themes, preferring to use love and nature for his inspiration, and wanted his poetry to be recognized on its own merits, not because of the color of the man who created it.

Cullen married Yolande Du Bois, the daughter of W.E.B. Du Bois, in 1928; they divorced only two years later. Cullen taught French and English in a New York junior high school for several years while continuing to write and publish poetry. He wrote a novel, *One Way to Heaven*, which was published in 1932 and, like Hughes, wrote several pieces for children. His writing appeared on Broadway, in a musical entitled *St. Louis Woman*, the result of a collaboration with Arna Bontemps. Cullen died in 1946, only a few months before the production opened.

Countee Cullen, like Langston Hughes, was an up-and-coming poet in Harlem during the 1920s. Though Hughes's and Cullen's styles and subjects differed, the two men became friends and encouraged each other's work.

Like Cullen, he carefully chose his language so it would fit the subject and emotion of his poems, but his poetry was not so formal in style.

Not only did their poetic styles differ, but the two poets also held differing views about the relationship between their race and their poetry. Hughes could not separate his interest in blacks from his desire to write poetry. He wrote about black people, black music, and black experiences while using black American speech rhymes and slang. Cullen considered himself to be a poet first and foremost, a poet who just happened to be black, so he did not center his poetry on his race. Instead, Cullen tended to write in a private voice about personal matters. In this way, he was almost the opposite of Hughes, who wrote in a boisterous voice about very public events: lynchings, jazz clubs, bill collectors, and the like. Despite these differences, the two men encouraged each other's work.

WEARY BLUES

Hughes's poems were steadily published throughout 1922. Cullen even read some of them as part of public readings held at the Harlem branch of the public library. Yet Hughes seemed to be struggling in his work. He was searching for a break-through that would raise his poetry to a higher level. That breakthrough came one night in March 1923, in a Harlem blues club, when he began writing "The Weary Blues." The poem perfectly expressed Hughes's desire to capture black music and speech in his poetry.

> Droning on a drowsy syncopated tune,
> Rocking back and forth to a mellow croon,
>   I heard a Negro play.
> Down on Lenox Avenue the other night
> By the pale dull pallor of an old gas light
>   He did a lazy sway. . . .
>   He did a lazy sway. . . .
> To the tune o' those Weary Blues.
> With his ebony hands on each ivory key
> He made the poor piano moan with melody.
>   O Blues!
> Swaying to and fro on his rickety stool

He played that sad raggy tune like a musical fool.
   Sweet Blues!
Coming from a black man's soul.
   O Blues!
In a deep song voice with a melancholy tone
I heard that Negro sing, that old piano moan—
   "Ain't got nobody in all this world,
   Ain't got nobody but ma self,
   I's gwine to quit ma frownin'
   And put ma troubles on the shelf."
Thump, thump, thump, went his foot on the floor.
He played a few chords then he sang some more—
   "I got the Weary Blues
   And I can't be satisfied.
   Got the Weary Blues
   And can't be satisfied—
   I ain't happy no mo'
   And I wish that I had died."
And far into the night he crooned that tune.
The stars went out and so did the moon.
The singer stopped playing and went to bed
While the Weary Blues echoed through his head.
He slept like a rock or a man that's dead.

What Hughes accomplished in this poem was new and remarkable. His use of rhythm and cadence, imitating black speech and blues music, was a brilliant coup. In writing "The Weary Blues," he took the sounds of street music and street talk and transformed them into a powerful and evocative voice all his own.

Hughes soon learned from Fauset that one of his poems was going to be published in an anthology entitled *Negro Poets and Their Poems*. This anthology was certain to give Hughes exposure to a larger audience. Fauset reminded him, "Hold fast to your dreams. . . ."

Art © Romare Bearden Foundation/Licensed by VAGA, New York, NY.

"Tenor Sermon" from the Jazz Series, 1979, by artist Romare Bearden. During the Harlem Renaissance in the 1920s, the uniquely black music styles of jazz and blues were growing in popularity. Hughes incorporated the rhythms and sounds of these styles into his poetry to create a voice that accurately represented the black experience.

Along with Cullen's and Fauset's support, Hughes also received encouragement from Alain Locke. The first black American to win a Rhodes scholarship, Locke had a quick mind and was vastly learned. He graduated magna cum laude in philosophy from Harvard, received a Rhodes scholarship to Oxford University in England, continued his graduate studies at the University of Berlin and the College de France, and then became a professor at Howard University in Washington, D.C. He wanted to assemble a group of intellectuals and writers who would enliven American culture, and he started to correspond with Hughes at his friend Cullen's suggestion.

In one of Locke's letters to Hughes, he suggested that Hughes, Cullen, and Jean Toomer (another promising young black writer, who was the author of *Cane*) work together on common projects. Hughes responded that he was interested in forming a small literary circle, although at the moment he was more interested in traveling, especially to France. He was becoming restless in Jones Point. Locke suggested that Hughes join him and Cullen on a trip to Europe that summer, but Hughes declined the invitation, preferring to travel on his own.

On June 4, 1923, Hughes quit his job on the Hudson and came to New York to search for a ship that would take him to a distant place. Unlike his first search for work aboard a ship, this time he found what he was looking for. The ship was called the *West Hesseltine,* and its destination was Africa.

4

An African Adventure

The *West Hesseltine* was not a cruise ship by any stretch of the imagination. It was a rusty, old freighter ready to make the difficult and dangerous voyage to the west coast of Africa. Since the trip would not be an easy one, the captain of the *West Hesseltine* could not be choosy when selecting his crew: He felt lucky to have a crew at all. So when Hughes arrived at dockside with excellent letters of recommendation from his supervisor at Jones Point in hand, he was hired immediately.

The ship left New York on June 13, 1923. Hughes was excited to be on the open sea at last, heading for an exotic foreign land. Although the 1920s marked a time when only the wealthy could afford to travel abroad, Hughes was en route to one of the least-traveled continents of the world.

Africa is considered by many black Americans to be their mother continent. Particularly in the segregated America of the 1920s, there was a sense that life in Africa would offer blacks a kind of freedom that they could not experience in America. The belief that Africa was the black homeland and the lost black Eden to which Afro-Americans should return was the major theme of activist Marcus Garvey, who founded the first American chapter of the Universal Negro Improvement Association (UNIA) in 1917. The UNIA embraced the slogan "Back to Africa" and attempted to organize blacks who lived in the Western hemisphere in a mass exodus to Africa. The project aroused widespread interest among black Americans, but largely because of the size of the project, it ultimately failed. Hughes was aware of Garvey's activities, along with the efforts of his friend and mentor W.E.B. Du Bois to organize a Pan African Congress. The meeting of this congress consisted of blacks seeking to protest European colonialism in Africa. Neither Garvey nor Du Bois had ever been to Africa. Yet that was where Hughes was going.

During the first night of his voyage, Hughes unpacked his bags in his cabin. He then took the collection of books he had carried with him while he was in New York onto deck. Suddenly, he threw all of the books—except for Walt Whitman's *Leaves of Grass*—into the ocean. As he later wrote:

> It was like throwing a million bricks out of my heart—
> for it wasn't only the books that I wanted to throw
> away, but everything unpleasant and miserable out of
> my past: the memory of my father, the poverty and
> uncertainties of my mother's life, the stupidities of
> color-prejudice, black in a white world, the fear of not
> finding a job, the bewilderment of no one to talk to
> about things that trouble you, the feeling of always
> being controlled by others—by parents, employers, by
> some outer necessity not your own. All these things I
> wanted to throw away. To be free of.

During the summer of 1923, the *West Hesseltine* made 32 stops up and down the West African coast. Hughes's first

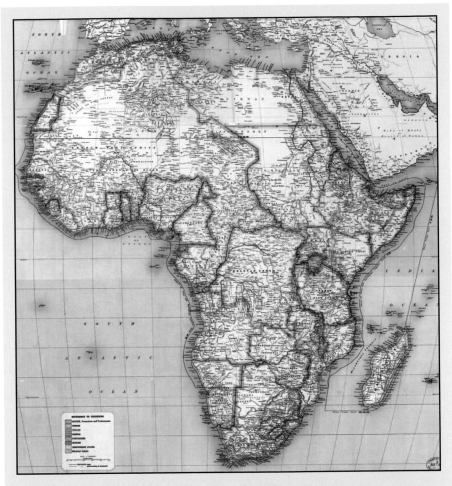

In an effort to see the world, Hughes joined the crew of a ship bound for Africa. Traveling along the west coast of Africa, he had many memorable and eye-opening experiences, some of which served as inspiration for his poems and short stories.

impressions of Africa were of its intense heat and the wild styles of dress of the people. Their dress ranged from near nakedness to unusual combinations, such as tribal robes worn with bowler hats. Gradually, Hughes saw through these surface impressions to the more important events that were occurring in Africa.

In Africa, nations did not exist in the usual sense of the term. The continent was a mixture of tribal cultures, although most of the tribes had already been influenced by the colonial powers of Europe, which exercised political control over almost all of the continent. Most of West Africa was divided between the British and the French, although tiny Belgium ruled the huge colony of the Belgian Congo (later called Zaire), and Portugal controlled the vast colony of Angola in southwest Africa.

Africa was not free politically, nor was it free economically. The African people were not allowed by their political masters in Europe to manufacture goods from their own raw materials. Materials such as palm oil, cocoa beans, and mahogany were shipped to Western countries, turned into various products, and then returned to Africa at a high price; the African people were given no jobs in producing these goods.

As the ship made its way slowly down the coast, from Senegal to Nigeria to the Cameroons (where Hughes crossed the equator for the first time and, according to custom, had his head shaved by the ship's crew), the tragedies of European colonialism were evident everywhere. The white traders and missionaries who had seized control of parts of Africa worked the African people very hard. Yet, to Hughes's surprise, many Africans still managed to live with a zest and grace that won his immediate respect and empathy.

Another surprise came when Hughes realized that the Africans whom he encountered did not think he was black. "The Africans looked at me and would not believe I was Negro," he said. "They looked at my copper-brown skin and straight black hair and they said: 'You—white man.'"

The voyage provided Hughes with similarly memorable encounters. In Port Harcourt, Nigeria, he met a boy who was the son of a white father and an African mother. The boy, who was light-skinned like Hughes, approached him and asked if it was true that people in America would talk to mulattoes like himself. In Africa, the boy explained, mulattoes were ignored by the native population. "He looked very lonely, as he stood on the dock the day our ship hauled anchor," Hughes said. "He had taken my address to write me in America, and once, a year later, I had a letter from him, but only one, because I have a way of not answering when I don't know what to say."

Such meetings benefited Hughes's writing. He published several short stories inspired by his trip. His poems "The White Ones" and "Dream Variation" were also written as a result of experiences he had in Africa.

The *West Hesseltine* went down the African coast to the Belgian Congo, then steamed up the Congo River for more than 100 miles to take on cargo. The poor Congo villages, with their taverns posting signs that said "Whites Only" and their patrols of armed black soldiers enforcing white colonial rules, depressed Hughes. The ship only remained at dock in the Congo for a few days before heading for Angola, the southernmost stop on the itinerary. The *West Hesseltine* proceeded to retrace its route back up the coast as far as Guinea, then started back home to New York.

FURTHER TRAVELS

With its hold full of African timber, copra (dried coconut meat), and other goods, the *West Hesseltine* returned to New York on October 21, 1923. Hughes was greeted as a returning hero by his friends from Harlem. They told him that an entire page of the August issue of *The Crisis* had been devoted to his poems and encouraged him to take an active part in Harlem's growing literary circle, which was headed chiefly by Fauset.

Hughes still wanted to see and know more of the world, so in December he shipped out on the *McKeesport* from Hoboken, New Jersey, to the Netherlands. Rotterdam was cold and white with snow when he arrived, and Hughes liked the whiteness, the narrow cobblestone streets of the city, and the cozy teahouses. He returned to Hoboken in late

January 1924, but when he was offered a return trip to Europe on the *McKeesport*, he took it. He left on his second European voyage a few days later on February 4, 1924.

During the voyage, Hughes thought of leaving the ship once it reached Rotterdam for an extended stay in Europe. When he got into an argument with the ship's steward a few days before they reached Holland, the disagreement helped Hughes to make up his mind. The day after the *McKeesport* landed in Rotterdam, he accepted his advance pay from the captain and used part of it to buy a train ticket to France.

Hughes arrived in Paris possessing only a few dollars and the names and addresses of two people. One of them— Claude McKay, the writer whom Hughes admired when he was a high school student in Cleveland—had just left Paris to live on the French Riviera. The other, a friend of Fauset's named Rayford Logan, told Hughes that he would see if he could find him a job.

Hughes rented a hotel room for his first night in Paris, then spent the next day looking for work at English-speaking establishments—the American Express office, the American library, and the U.S. embassy—without having any success. Within a few days Hughes finally managed to get himself hired—as a bouncer at a nightclub frequented by prostitutes and their drunken customers. Fights occurred often at the club, and when the first one erupted, Hughes fled into the night.

Luckily for Hughes, Fauset's friend Logan soon came through with a job offer, and Hughes was hired as a dishwasher at a popular nightclub, Le Grand Duc. The club was partially owned by an American, Eugene Ballard, who had been the only black pilot to fly in the Lafayette Flying Corps during World War I. The American-type club offered Southern-style cooking, plenty of wine, and—what made it especially popular with the Parisians—American jazz.

Hughes went to the club every evening at eleven and worked past the closing time, which was three in the morning. From three until the sun came up a floating group of musicians would drift in and out of the club to play in all-night jam sessions. The stars of the club were the singers Florence Jones and Ada Beatrice Queen Victoria Louisa Virginia Smith (known more informally as Bricktop). Pianist Palmer Jones, trumpeter Cricket Smith, and drummer Buddy Gilmore were among the musicians who showed up for the jam sessions.

Shortly after spring arrived in Paris, Hughes met Anne Coussey. Part Scot and part African, she had been educated in England, and she had come to Paris to study French. Hughes was immediately attracted to her, and he soon began spending many of his afternoons at her apartment in the Latin Quarter of Paris. Their relationship proceeded to the point where Coussey asked Hughes whether he would consider marrying her, even though she had received a proposal of marriage from someone in London. Hughes told her that he was not interested in marriage because it would interfere with his life as a poet. Their relationship grew strained after this exchange. Coussey eventually left Paris—and Hughes's life—in the late spring.

One morning during the summer of 1924, Alain Locke arrived in Paris. He knew through Countee Cullen that Hughes was in the city, and he paid Hughes a visit in order to meet him for the first time and to present him with two proposals. The first was that Hughes submit some poetry for a special issue on blacks for *Graphic Survey* magazine, which Locke was going to edit. The second was that Hughes travel with Locke to Italy.

Hughes had already been invited to Italy by two Italian brothers who were waiters at Le Grand Duc. Like most business establishments in Paris, the club was closing for the month of August. Hughes arranged to meet Locke in Verona, Italy, after he visited the two brothers.

During Hughes's trip to Italy, he got along well with Locke, who proposed that if Hughes were ever to enroll at Howard University, he should stay with him. Yet as they traveled

Hughes lived in Paris, France, for several months, working at the popular night club, Le Grande Duc. He spent his nights with the musicians who came through the club for jam sessions, including the well-known singer and club owner Madame Duconge, or "Bricktop," seen here in 1959.

together, a strain developed in their relationship—one that became apparent when Hughes and Locke were planning to depart for America from the port of Genoa. On the train from Venice to Genoa, Hughes was robbed while he was sleeping. For reasons that have never been made clear, Locke did little to help out Hughes other than lend him a small amount of money. Locke then departed for America while Hughes, stranded in Genoa, was forced to live at a settlement house for down-and-out sailors.

With barely enough money to live on, Hughes kept trying to get a job on a ship bound for America, but his efforts met with no success. Hughes suspected prejudice was the cause. As he saw white sailors find work aboard ships without much difficulty, he become more and more downcast, particularly because he had grown desperate for money. In such a depressed frame of mind, he wrote "I, Too, Sing America," one of his most powerful and best-known poems.

I, too, sing America.

I am the darker brother.
They send me to eat in the kitchen
When company comes,
But I laugh,
And eat well,
And grow strong.

Tomorrow,
I'll sit at the table
When company comes.
Nobody'll dare
Say to me,
"Eat in the kitchen,"
Then.
Besides,
They'll see how beautiful I am
And be ashamed,—
I, too, am America.

Hughes was finally forced to send a frantic request to the *Crisis* staff in New York for financial assistance. Although the money never arrived, a ship willing to take him on soon did. The ship was the *West Cawthon*, bound for New York and staffed by an all-black crew.

Hughes later explained this harrowing ordeal with characteristic good humor. "The months before," he said, "I had got to Paris with seven dollars. I had been in France, Italy, and Spain. And after the Grand Tour of the Mediterranean, I came home with a quarter, so my . . . European trip cost me exactly six dollars and seventy-five cents."

5

In Vogue

Hughes returned from Europe in November 1924 to discover that the Harlem Renaissance was flourishing. During the 10 months that he had been gone, several black writers—including Jessie Fauset—had been published by major presses, indirectly helping all black writers to gain a wider reading audience. A new magazine, called *Opportunity*, was published by the National Urban League and edited by Charles Johnson. Along with the *Messenger*, which was edited by the labor leader A. Philip Randolph, *Opportunity* gave black writers another prestigious place to publish their work besides *The Crisis*.

Chief among the Harlem-based writers who saw their reputations beginning to grow was Hughes himself. Many of his poems, including "Dream Variation" and "Grant Park" were appearing in different magazines and journals. So when Hughes attended a benefit party for the NAACP on the night of his return from Europe, he was greeted warmly and as a well-respected peer by such eminent black writers as Walter White and James Weldon Johnson.

Unlike his first arrival in New York, this time Hughes did not think it was so important to be in the middle of Harlem's cultural excitement. In early 1925, he moved to Washington, D.C. He planned to attend Howard University and to be with his mother and stepbrother Gwyn, who were living in the nation's capital.

They were staying with wealthy relatives of Carrie's uncle, John Mercer Langston. Long deceased by the time Hughes moved to Washington, John Mercer Langston had made a name for himself in the Civil War and Reconstruction eras as a clerk of an Ohio township, then as inspector-general of the Freedman's Bureau, the agency created by the federal government to protect ex-slaves after the end of the Civil War. He later was appointed ambassador to Haiti and ended his political career as a congressman from Virginia.

Hughes's Washington relatives were excessively proud people who lived in an elite and exclusive world. Because his mother came to Washington without money or social standing, they treated her with little respect. Hughes was dealt with more carefully by his relatives. He was, after all, an author who was published by respected magazines. Still, he disturbed them with his stories of shipping out on old freighters and washing dishes in Paris jazz bars, for these were activities of which they did not approve. Shortly after Hughes took a job in a steam laundry, he moved with his mother and Gwyn into a rooming house in an unfashionable neighborhood, far from the swank streets where their Washington relatives lived.

Once Hughes had moved to a neighborhood that he found more suitable, he started spending more time at blues clubs and streetcorner joints. Hughes drew inspiration from these places. "I tried to write poems like the songs they sang on Seventh Street," he said. These songs "had the pulse beat of the people who keep on going."

When he returned to the United States in 1925, Hughes took several different jobs, including working as a busboy, to support himself. He drew inspiration from the experiences and people he encountered, and began to mold his writing style after the speech patterns and attitudes of the people he met.

Among the poems that Hughes wrote during this time were "The Cat and the Saxophone" and "Railroad Avenue." With their syncopated sounds and free-form lines, these works were further refinements of Hughes's blues and jazz poetry. Much as a cubist painter will take a realistic, recognizable figure and change it into a series of cubic blocks to indicate depth and movement, so Hughes arranged single words and short phrases on a page to convey a sense of motion and life.

Although Hughes's creative output in Washington was high, he was still doing lowly and unsatisfying labor. After working at the laundry for a brief period, he got a job at an oyster house, and then he was employed as an assistant to Dr. Carter Woodson, the editor of the *Journal of Negro History*. Woodson had received a large grant from both the Carnegie and Rockefeller Foundations to establish a publishing company devoted to the study of Afro-Americans. He hired Hughes to help prepare one of the first volumes of this study entitled *Free Negro Heads of Families in the United States in 1830*. Hughes admired Woodson and his work, but he found his own job of proofreading and alphabetizing 30,000 names to be rather tedious. Nonetheless, he needed the money, so he remained with Dr. Woodson in Washington through most of 1925.

Hughes returned briefly to New York in May 1925 to attend a banquet sponsored by Charles Johnson and *Opportunity* magazine. The banquet was held to give out awards and monetary prizes as part of a literary contest to determine the best black writers in America. The contest was judged by a panel of distinguished American writers and publishers, including Robert Benchley, Eugene O'Neill, and Alexander Woolcott. The contest was divided into different literary categories, and Hughes's main rival in the poetry contest was Countee Cullen, whose work was becoming extremely popular with both blacks and whites.

A star-studded, glittering affair, the awards dinner proved to be an important night for the 23-year-old Hughes. His poem "The Weary Blues," written two years before but still unpublished, won first prize and was read aloud to the banquet audience by James Weldon Johnson. Among the people with whom Hughes became acquainted that night was Carl Van Vechten, a writer and critic. One of the few whites in New

The Cotton Club was the most famous and exclusive jazz club in Harlem during the 1920s and 1930s. Though the club had a whites-only policy for patrons, it was known for showcasing the best black performers of the day, including Cab Calloway, Duke Ellington, and Dorothy Dandridge.

York to investigate the Harlem that existed outside the whites-only jazz clubs (such as the Cotton Club), Van Vechten was intensely interested in the new artistic movements that were developing in New York. A critic whose words appeared in many influential magazines, he had begun to champion various black artists, including the actor and singer Paul Robeson. Van Vechten and his wife also invited black and white artists, writers, publishers, and agents to parties in their home, attempting to bring blacks and whites together in New York.

Over the next two weeks, Van Vechten worked with Hughes on editing his poetry. Then, during a lunch with his own publisher, Alfred Knopf, Van Vechten presented Hughes's poetry to Knopf and recommended that he publish Hughes's work. Knopf quickly agreed. A mere 17 days after the *Opportunity* dinner in New York, Hughes signed a contract for the publication of his first work of collected poems, *The Weary Blues*. Van Vechten wrote the introduction to the book, and the Mexican artist Miguel Covarrubias designed the cover.

Hughes was astonished with Van Vechten's clout. He was also ecstatic. He wrote Van Vechten, "As the old folks say, I'll have to walk sideways to keep from flying."

Yet this was not the end of Van Vechten's promotion of Hughes. Van Vechten wrote articles about black arts and culture for the popular magazine *Vanity Fair* and arranged for several of Hughes's poems to appear in one of its issues. "Never in

IN HIS OWN WORDS...

While Langston Hughes was living in Washington, D.C., and working for Carter Woodson, he continued to write and publish poetry. He also maintained a correspondence with Carl Van Vechten, and his letters give insight to Hughes's daily life during this period, as this excerpt from a letter to Van Vechten, written on May 7, 1925, reveals:

Dear Carl,
What a delightful surprise, your letter! I didn't think you would write me first as I've had you in mind all week for a note. I typed "Frankie Baker" for you on Monday but have been waiting for a chance to write a few explanations about it. I've been busy.

Perhaps you have heard "Frankie" before. It's a very old song, and is supposed to have originated in Omaha after Frankie Baker, a colored sporting-woman famous in the West, had shot her lover, Albert. The whole song runs to a blues tune, the chorus very blue, but the tune of each verse varies slightly, better to express the sentiment. . . .

I am going to rearrange the book Sunday. I can work on poetry only when it amuses me, and this week it didn't amuse me. I was too sleepy. . . .

my wildest dreams had I imagined a chance at *Vanity Fair*," Hughes said.

Hughes's sudden success in the publishing world created a flurry of excitement among his friends in Harlem. His success did not change the circumstances of his life, however. He continued to work for Dr. Woodson in Washington, and he still shared the same two-room apartment with his mother and stepbrother. He hoped that his publishing success would help him get a scholarship to Howard University, especially because he could no longer depend on the influence of Alain Locke, who had been fired from the Howard faculty because of his involvement in a student strike. Hughes applied for a scholarship to the university but was turned down.

THE POET AND THE BUSBOY

In the fall of 1925, Hughes moved out of his family's apartment and quit his job with Dr. Woodson. Supported by the small amount of money he had received from *Vanity Fair*, an advance payment from his publisher, Knopf, and some money from Van Vechten, he tried for a few months to write an autobiography, something that Van Vechten had encouraged him to do. Hughes lived in a room at Washington's 12th Street YMCA, but the writing went slowly and with difficulty. He was not yet ready to write the story of his life—except as it might appear in his poetry. Worried about his future and wondering whether he would ever return to college, he moved back in with his mother and took a job as a busboy at the Wardman Park Hotel.

Hughes was working in the restaurant of the hotel in late November when Vachel Lindsay, one of America's best-known poets, visited the hotel to give a poetry reading. Recognizing Lindsay in the restaurant from his picture in the morning newspaper, Hughes thought of introducing himself but shyness got the better of him. Instead of saying anything, Hughes "wrote out three of my poems on some pieces of paper and put them in the pocket of my white bus boy's coat. In the evening when Mr. Lindsay came down to dinner, quickly I laid them beside his plate and went away, afraid to say anything to so famous a poet, except that I liked his poems and these were poems of mine."

During Lindsay's reading that night, he announced to his audience that he had discovered a promising young black poet and then proceeded to read aloud all three of the poems that Hughes had left for him. The next day, members of the press surrounded Hughes, photographing him at the hotel in his busboy's uniform and asking him about himself. By the end of the month, the story about Hughes and Lindsay had been picked up by the Associated Press wire service and was carried all over the country. The episode was all the publicity Hughes needed to launch the publication of *The Weary Blues* in January 1926.

Although Hughes's literary career was on the rise, he was still anxious to go to college. Late in October 1925, he had applied and been admitted to Lincoln University, a small, all-black school not far from Philadelphia, Pennsylvania. Hughes could not count on attending college until he found enough money to pay for three years of schooling. After attending a November party in his honor at Van Vechten's apartment in New York (a party, he noted, that none of the black leadership in Washington had ever thought to give him), he met Amy Spingarn, the daughter of a wealthy industrialist. Spingarn, her husband, and her brother-in-law were all deeply involved in the struggle for racial equality in New York; they donated generously to the NAACP and many other black organizations. (For additional information on the Spingarn family's legacy, enter "Amy Spingarn" into any search engine and browse the sites listed.)

Hughes explained to Amy Spingarn that he wanted to finish his university education but that he did not have the money to do so. He further explained that even though most of his friends were urging him to attend an Ivy League school, preferably Harvard, he wanted to go to Lincoln. He described his experiences at Columbia, then told her he was searching for someone who could help him out financially. Spingarn

Vachel Lindsay

Hughes's encounter with poet Vachel Lindsay in November 1925, when Hughes was working as a busboy at the Wardman Park Hotel, made headlines in newspapers all over the country. The praise of Hughes' writing by Lindsay, one of America's best-known poets of the time, helped publicize Hughes's *The Weary Blues* when it was published only two months after his encounter with Lindsay.

Vachel Lindsay was born on November 10, 1879, in Springfield, Illinois. His given name was Nicholas Vachel Lindsay. He attended Hiram College in Ohio from 1897 to 1899 but never earned a degree. Instead he focused on writing—writing in notebooks and diaries and eventually writing poetry. His writing was heavily influenced by his own philosophy of what he believed was an almost spiritual role that art could play in shaping mankind. Lindsay attended the Chicago Art Institute and the New York School of Art before he decided to focus on poetry as his artistic medium.

Lindsay's early years were spent in self-printing and marketing his poetry, first peddling poems in the streets of New York and then later speaking out on the issues of race and prohibition while selling his poetry in Springfield. In 1912, Lindsay decided to walk to Los Angeles and then to Seattle before returning to Springfield, carrying his poems for sale. He got no farther than New Mexico before taking a train to Los Angeles, where he wrote "General William Booth Enters Heaven," a poem written to honor the founder of the Salvation Army, which was published in *Poetry* in 1913. This poem made him famous; his recitations of his poems made him infamous. Lindsay had a habit of singing and shouting his poetry while rocking back and forth on his feet and pumping his arms. His belief was that, by making poetry entertaining, he was able to expose a wider audience to the art form he loved. Lindsay traveled throughout the United States and England for many years. Despite his fame, he suffered constant financial difficulties.

Later in life, Lindsay was diagnosed with epilepsy and struggled with paranoia. He married in 1925 and had two children, but mental illness made his family life unstable. He committed suicide at home on December 5, 1931.

did not make any promises to him, although she did say that she would keep his dilemma in mind. The day before Christmas Hughes received a letter in Washington. Spingarn would underwrite his education. He should choose a school to his liking and enroll immediately. "It was the happiest holiday gift I've ever received," said Hughes. "My poems— through the kindness of this woman who liked poetry—sent me to college."

Hughes entered Lincoln University in February 1926. Along with Lincoln's reputation for academic excellence—the students referred to it as "the black Princeton"—Hughes elected to study there because the school was only a train ride away from New York. Although he worked diligently at Lincoln, he made frequent, and sometimes extended, visits to Manhattan. He did not want to miss out on what he called "the period when the Negro was in vogue."

After Hughes's first semester of school ended, he spent the summer of 1926 in Harlem living in the same apartment building as his friend Wallace Thurman. The two of them headed a group of young black artists who began to spend a lot of time with one another. The other artists in the group included Zora Neale Hurston, a writer and folklorist then studying at Columbia University; the painter Aaron Douglas; actor and writer Bruce Nugent, whom Hughes knew from Washington; and the poet and artist Gwendolyn Bennett, just back from studying in Europe. Hurston called this group the "Niggerati."

Hughes had a fair amount of money coming in that summer —he began to receive royalties for *The Weary Blues*, payment for a magazine article he had written, and the winnings from another poetry prize—so he was able to spend a good deal of the summer concentrating on his poetry. He also devoted a lot of his energy to writing lyrics and scenes for a black musical revue that had been proposed by Caroline Reagan, a friend of Van Vechten's. The play was to be called *0 Blues!* and was supposed to star Paul Robeson. Hughes's work on the play was interrupted by his teaming up with Hurston to write the plot, dialogue, and lyrics for a black opera. This project, too, faltered after a while.

The Niggerati did succeed in completing one of their works: the publication of a one-issue magazine called *Fire!!* According to Hughes, it was published to "burn up a lot of the old, dead conventional Negro–white ideas of the past." It was also supposed to counter the reaction of the black bourgeoisie to some of Hughes's earthy blues poems, as well as the critical savaging by middle-class blacks of Carl Van Vechten's new novel, *Nigger Heaven*. Hurston, Hughes, Nugent, and Thurman hoped that *Fire!!* would provide young black artists with a place to publish their work. The magazine was almost not issued because the Niggerati could not raise enough cash to pay their printer. Van Vechten finally loaned them enough money to ensure its publication. The magazine was met with outraged condemnation. "None of the older Negro intellectuals would have anything to do with *Fire!!*" Hughes said. The Niggerati thus succeeded in provoking a response with *Fire!!* but they never managed to put together enough money to print more than one issue.

INDELICATE POETRY

In the fall of 1926, Hughes was back at Lincoln University, editing and paring his latest poems into a book-length manuscript. When he had finished his editing, he sent the poems to Van Vechten, who submitted the manuscript to Knopf. The poems were published in February 1927 under the title *Fine Clothes to the Jew*. Although protests were made about the title being anti-Semitic, it was actually taken from a poem in the collection that described hard times. In this poem, Hughes sought to make use of the stereotype of Jews as pawnbrokers, people whose services would be in demand when times grew hard.

The poems in *Fine Clothes to the Jew* offered as earthy and unsentimental a description of black life as had then been published. The poems did not present a falsely pretty picture of black life. Several of the characters were drunks and prostitutes. Sex and violence were among the themes incorporated into the poetry. Hughes wrote about the darker side of black life, partly because it attracted him and partly because it existed and so few others had written about it. "My poems are indelicate," he admitted. "But so is life."

Several leading members of the black press attacked *Fine Clothes to the Jew* for presenting a negative view of blacks to the world. The *Amsterdam News* in New York reviewed it under the headline "Sewer Dweller"; the *Pittsburgh Courier* called it "piffling trash." Hughes replied by pointing out that he was not the first to write about such characters. He said, "Solomon, Homer, Shakespeare, and Walt Whitman were not afraid to include them."

In mid-April 1927, a few months after the publication of *Fine Clothes to the Jew*, Hughes met a woman in her 70s who in time would have an important, almost crushing effect on his life. Her name was Charlotte Mason, and she was introduced to him through Alain Locke. The widow of a well-known psychologist and physician, Mason was an heiress to generations of wealth. Her Park Avenue apartment, which afforded a dramatic view of Manhattan, was filled with exquisite collections of European, African, and American Indian art.

Having been told by Locke that Hughes was an up-and-coming poet, Mason summoned Hughes to her apartment to tell him about her hope of fostering black art and writing. She believed that blacks, like Indians, were "primitive people" who were in closer contact with nature and their natural impulses than were whites. She insisted that she did not mean this as an insult, but as praise. Her mission, she told Hughes, was to save the world—at least to save those things that were natural and spontaneous in the world—by making the art and writing of blacks better known. "As the fire burned in me," she said, "I had the mystical vision of a great bridge reaching from Harlem to the heart of Africa, across which the Negro world, that our white United States had done everything to annihilate, should see the flaming pathway . . . and recover the treasures their people had had in the beginning of African life on earth." Hughes said of her, "I found her instantly one of the most delightful women I had ever met, witty and charming, kind and sympathetic."

Mason wanted Hughes (as well as Locke and Hurston) to help her realize her vision. She would give him money to support his work, and he would acknowledge her guidance in the direction his work would take. For Hughes, who had been poor all his life, her offer was one he could not afford to turn down.

In addition to the need for financial help, there was something in Hughes's emotional makeup that responded deeply to Mason. Shortly after their first meeting—and after Mason began to be Hughes's patron—she requested that he not call her "Mrs. Mason" but "Godmother." Hughes agreed. He maintained, "No one else had ever been so thoughtful of me, or so interested in the things I wanted to do, or so kind and generous toward me."

After Hughes's first semester at Lincoln ended in May, he left on a tour of the South. He read some of his poems at Fisk University in Nashville, Tennessee, then continued farther south to Memphis, Tennessee, and New Orleans, Louisiana. This poetry-reading tour was the first of many he was to give (in his later years, such tours would become an important way for him to support himself). It was also his first trip to the South. He viewed the trip as an opportunity not only to make some money with his readings, but also to get to know Southern blacks better.

From New Orleans, Hughes took a small freighter to Havana, Cuba, for a brief stay. He then returned to New Orleans and started traveling north, stopping off at Mobile, Alabama. Walking down the main street in Mobile, he unexpectedly encountered Zora Neale Hurston, who was driving around the South for the summer, collecting field notes for her mentor, the anthropologist Franz Boas of Columbia University. Hughes and Hurston traveled north together, visiting Tuskegee Institute, founded by Booker T. Washington, in Tuskegee, Alabama; rushing over to Macon, Georgia, to catch a performance of the legendary blues singer Bessie Smith; and visiting the isolated, rural black churches.

The summer of 1927 proved to be a rare carefree time for Hughes. In the years that were to follow, he would not have many happy periods like this one again.

6

A Fall From Grace

Shortly after the fall semester of 1927 began at Lincoln, Hughes traveled to Manhattan to see Charlotte Mason. He was presented with a concrete proposal of financial support that would last for the next three years. He would be paid $150 a month so that he would not have to worry about anything other than his writing. If he wanted to travel for purposes of literary investigation, she would pay his expenses on top of his regular monthly stipend.

Hughes gratefully accepted Mason's offer. Once he had taken on her support, however, his life and work began to change. His poetry decreased in both quality and output. Perhaps Hughes had simply exhausted his creative abilities for a while; after all, he had just published two full volumes of poetry, and he was devoting much of his time to a semiautobiographical novel about a lonely, young black boy's passage from childhood to maturity. Yet something else was influencing his work as well.

By patronizing Hughes, Mason—no matter how noble her intentions—was helping to deprive the poet of the emotional intensity he needed to produce truly inspired work.

The psychological relationship between Hughes and Mason grew tangled. He developed a deep affection for her that went far beyond mere gratitude for the financial support she offered. For Hughes, Mason became something like a second mother. The emotional support she gave him—the feeling of being cared for, of not being alone anymore—kept him coming back to her apartment for long afternoons of conversation. Hughes said:

> Out of a past of more or less continued insecurity and fear, suddenly I found myself with an assured income from someone who loved and believed in me, an apartment in a suburban village for my work, my brother in school in New England and no longer a financial difficulty to my mother, myself with boxes of fine bond paper for writing, a filing case, a typist to copy my work, and wonderful new suits of dinner clothes from Fifth Avenue shops, and a chance to go to all the theater and operas and lectures, no matter how expensive or difficult securing tickets might be. All I needed to say was when and where I wished to go and my patron's secretary would have tickets for me.

Growing accustomed to the finer things in life, Hughes saw his enthusiasm for academics decrease during 1927 and 1928. He wrote the lyrics of a song for W.C. Handy, the preeminent blues composer. He authored a few sonnets as well as some mild social protests for the socialist magazine *New Masses.* He had to be careful with his poems of social protest, however, because Charlotte Mason hated socialism. (For additional information on composer W.C. Handy, enter "WC Handy" into any search engine and browse the sites listed.)

In the summer of 1928, Hughes went into seclusion in a rented apartment near Lincoln and continued working on his novel about a young man coming of age. The story was set in Kansas, where Hughes had spent the earliest part of his childhood. He finished the first draft in the fall and dutifully sent a copy to his godmother. Mason liked parts of the story but urged him to begin a second draft. The revision proved to be a difficult task. Hughes felt uncomfortable when writing long works of fiction, and his godmother's scrutiny inhibited him. During the academic year that began in 1928—his senior year at Lincoln University—he worked on the second draft of the novel as often as his schoolwork and his forays into Manhattan would allow him.

After graduating from Lincoln University in the spring of 1929, Hughes took a room—at Charlotte Mason's urging—in the quiet, residential town of Westfield, New Jersey, which was about an hour's travel from Manhattan. He hired Louise Thompson, who had been married briefly to Hughes's friend Wallace Thurman, to type for him, and he began to work steadily on the novel, without spending as much time as usual in Manhattan.

By then, Hughes's friends in the Niggerati had left Harlem. Bruce Nugent was in London working as an actor, Zora Neale Hurston was in the South working on her field notes for her dissertation, and Wallace Thurman was in Hollywood, trying to earn a living as a writer. They had all seen Harlem change since its glory days only a few years before. Whereas the people who lived in Harlem in the mid-1920s were filled with hope and optimism, by the late 1920s feelings of boredom and weariness had set in. The crash of the New York Stock Exchange on October 24 would add to this somber mood and downward slide and seal Harlem's fate as an economically depressed area.

By the summer of 1929, Hughes was ready to claim, "I've never felt so unpoetic in my life. I suppose I'm not quite miserable enough. I usually have to feel very bad in order to put anything down." He continued with a third revision of the novel, which he named *Not Without Laughter*, through the fall of 1929. He finally finished it just before Christmas, and the novel was published in early 1930.

Admired for its depiction of ordinary black life, *Not Without Laughter* received a tremendous amount of praise. Among its admirers was the *Pittsburgh Courier*, which had disapproved of Hughes's previous book. The newspaper now stated, "Bring out the laurel wreath and drape the brow of Langston Hughes."

A SINGING PLAY

Hughes's next project was to resume work on a folk opera, which he called a "singing play." He began searching for a

Zora Neale Hurston

Zora Neale Hurston shared Langston Hughes's view that blackness was something to be celebrated, and much of Hurston's writing reflects this view of the positive aspects of being a black American. For 30 years, from the 1930s through the 1960s, Hurston published seven books, numerous short stories, magazine articles, and plays.

Much of the details of Hurston's childhood were unclear, even to her. She frequently gave her birth date as January 7, 1903; later records revealed that she was born in 1891. She was the fifth of eight children born to Lucy Ann Potts, a schoolteacher, and John Hurston, a carpenter and Baptist teacher. Her early years were spent in Eatonville, Florida, an all-black community of which her father served as mayor for three terms.

Hurston's mother died in 1904, and Zora then spent several years living with one relative after another, when her father and his second wife refused to have her live with them. When she was 14, Hurston left home for good, working as a maid and traveling around the South and eventually earning her high school diploma. In the fall of 1918, she entered Howard University, attending classes part time for several years while working as a maid and manicurist. Her writing was published in Howard's magazine, *Stylus*.

By January 1925, Hurston was in New York, where she encountered Hughes and others involved in the Harlem Renaissance. Hurston's stories were soon

composer to work with his lyrics but was unable to find anyone suitable in New York. He decided to travel to Cuba, where
he could research Afro-Caribbean and Latin American music.
Mason thought that doing such research was a wonderful idea
and provided him with the money for the trip.

Hughes arrived in Havana in late February, shortly after
his 28th birthday, and promptly introduced himself to Jose
Antonio Fernández de Castro, the editor of Havana's principal
newspaper. Fernández de Castro had translated some of
Hughes's poetry into Spanish. Through him, Hughes met a
number of the leading young Cuban poets, including Nicolás
Guillén, who would soon become famous in the Spanish-
speaking world for accomplishing much the same thing that

being published in influential magazines such as *Opportunity*. Hurston's writing
was marked by strong, independent female characters and the use of rural
black dialect. She eventually won a scholarship to Barnard, where she met
Franz Boas, a professor at Columbia. Under Boas, Hurston began studying
anthropology and embarked on a study of African-American lore.

Much of the material she collected would help shape her stories and
musical plays. Her first novel, *Jonah's Gourd Vine*, was published in 1934
and received favorable reviews. In 1935, she was awarded a Guggenheim
Fellowship to collect folklore in the West Indies. Her travels through the
Caribbean would inspire her to write—in only seven weeks—*Their Eyes
Were Watching God*, a novel that is still considered a classic of American
twentieth-century literature.

Hurston continued to write fiction, an autobiography, and numerous
magazine articles. Later novels would not experience the success of her
early works, and by the 1950s she was nearly penniless, working at various
times as a maid, a librarian, and a substitute teacher. She suffered a stroke
on October 29, 1959 and died in a welfare nursing home on January 28,
1960, in Fort Pierce, Florida. More than 20 years after her death, a new
generation of writers such as Alice Walker and Toni Morrison would cite
Hurston's influence, and her writing would once more receive critical attention.

Hughes had done in English: using native rhythms (in Guillén's case, Afro-Cuban rhythms) and speech in poetry while confronting the problems of racism along with European and American imperialism.

Fernández de Castro and Guillén helped Hughes with his "singing play" project by taking him to many of the well-known music clubs in Havana, where Hughes heard the percussive, Afro-Cuban music called son. He decided to use this music for his opera, but he still had trouble finding the right person to compose it. He finally gave up on his search for a composer and returned to New York in early March. He felt refreshed from his trip, but he was still without a clear feeling of what he should do next. Charlotte Mason saw to it that he did not have to look far for answers.

Like Hughes, Zora Neale Hurston also had Mason for a patron. At the elderly woman's request, Hurston moved to Westfield, New Jersey, into a house not far from where Hughes lived. Soon the two began working together on a play called *Mule Bone*, based on the myths and folkstyles of rural Southern blacks. They had nearly finished the play when things started to go very wrong between Hughes and his patron.

The only poems that Hughes was able to complete after his return from Cuba dealt with his feelings of guilt mingled with anger. Thanks to Mason's money, he was able to lead a comfortable life while others were suffering through the hardships of the great economic depression that followed the stock market crash. Hughes's feelings emerged in poems such as "Advertisement for the Waldorf-Astoria," which parodied an advertisement for the new and socially exclusive Waldorf-Astoria Hotel in New York.

Unable to complete any long-term projects, including his singing play, Hughes began to disappoint Mason with his lack of productivity. She felt that he was spending too much of his time socializing with Hurston and too little of his time working hard. When Mason told him of her disappointment,

A view from a café in Havana, the capital of Cuba, around 1930. After publishing his acclaimed novel, *Not Without Laughter*, in 1930, Hughes spent time in Cuba socializing with fellow poets and artists and doing research to prepare for writing a folk opera, or "singing play."

Hughes believed that she was trying to exercise control over his writing. He told her, "So far in this world, only my writing has been my own, to do when I wanted to do it, to finish only when I felt it was finished, to put it aside or discard it completely if I chose . . . nobody ever said to me 'you must write now. You must finish that poem tomorrow. You must begin to create on the first of the month.'" While he resented her attempted increase in authority, she accused Hughes of being ungrateful to her. Much to Hughes's disappointment, their friendship—and their financial arrangement—collapsed.

Depressed at the thought of losing the support of the one person who understood "how I must battle the darkness within my self," Hughes turned to writing despondent poems, such as "Dear Lovely Death":

Dear lovely Death
That taketh all things under wing—
Never to kill—
Only to change
Into some other thing
This suffering flesh,
To make it either more or less,
Yet not again the same—
Dear lovely Death,
Change is thy other name.

After trying and failing to have a meeting of reconciliation with Charlotte Mason, Hughes finally realized that their relationship was over. In late December 1930 he left Westfield to join his mother in Cleveland. While there, he gave a poetry reading for the students and teachers at his old high school. He also discovered by coincidence that *Mule Bone*, the play he and Hurston had collaborated on, had been copyrighted in Hurston's name only and was being offered as a production for theater groups. Hughes was surprised at Hurston's greediness and confronted her about her claiming sole credit for the play. He made her agree to a settlement but this incident severed their friendship.

CARIBBEAN REVIVAL

During this struggle with Hurston, Hughes was awarded the Harmon Prize for achievement in black literature. The prize money was a relatively large sum for Hughes, $400, and he used this money to finance a trip in April 1931 to Cuba and Haiti. In Cuba, Hughes visited friends and revived himself under the warm Caribbean sun. He then sailed to Haiti, where he made a pilgrimage to the fortress of La Ferrière, a citadel built atop a mountain in the country's rugged interior. The citadel had been established by the nineteenth-century revolutionary leaders Toussaint L'Ouverture, Jean-Jacques Dessalines, and Henri Christophe, who were part of a generation of black Haitians who successfully rebelled against Haiti's French colonial rulers. These men had helped Haiti to become the world's first black republic.

The ruins of the fortress and of the Sans Souci palace in the jungle below it represented to Hughes more than just the decline of a mighty black power. The sight of these ruins reminded him of his own fall from grace and affected him deeply. It renewed his sense of purpose. As Hughes put it, "When I was twenty-seven the stock-market crash came.

IN HIS OWN WORDS...

In 1926, Langston Hughes shared his thoughts on the challenges facing African-American artists of his time in an essay published in *The Nation* titled "The Negro Artist and the Racial Mountain." Hughes addressed the conflict many of his peers faced in trying to develop an art independent of consideration of their race, as this excerpt reveals:

Certainly there is, for the American Negro artist who can escape the restrictions the more advanced among his own group would put upon him, a great field of unused material ready for his art. Without going outside his race, and even among the better classes with their "white" culture and conscious American manners, but still Negro enough to be different, there is sufficient matter to furnish a black artist with a lifetime of creative work. And when he chooses to touch on the relations between Negroes and whites in this country, with their innumerable overtones and undertones surely, and especially for literature and the drama, there is an inexhaustible supply of themes at hand. To these the Negro artist can give his racial individuality, his heritage of rhythm and warmth, and his incongruous humor that so often, as in the Blues, becomes ironic laughter mixed with tears.

The Haitian fortress of La Ferrière was established in the nineteenth century by black revolutionary leaders in their successful quest to make Haiti the world's first black republic. Hughes's trip to Haiti renewed his sense of purpose and his desire to write, though the injustices he witnessed made him pessimistic and politically radical.

When I was twenty-eight, my personal crash came. Then I guess I woke up."

Although Hughes felt a sense of renewal amid the ruins in Haiti, he was disturbed by some of this black republic's other sights. "It was in Haiti," he said, "that I first realized how class lines may cut across color lines within a race, and how dark people of the same nationality may scorn those below them."

Toward the end of Hughes's stay in Haiti, he met Jacques Roumain, an important innovator in third-world literature. Like Hughes (and Guillén in Cuba), Roumain was using his poetry to explore the folk motifs of his native land. Hughes and Roumain enjoyed one another's company immensely and began a lifelong friendship.

In July, after having been gone from the United States for three months, Hughes left the Caribbean to return to New York. While traveling up the East Coast from Florida to New York, he stopped at Bethune-Cookman College in Daytona Beach, Florida, to meet Mary McLeod Bethune, the college's president. Her suggestion that he give a reading tour of his poems in the South stayed in his mind as he headed north—with the famous educator as an unexpected traveling companion.

Hughes's trip to the Caribbean helped him to gather his thoughts, although it had not left him particularly optimistic that all of the injustices in the world would ever be corrected. For a time he had thought otherwise. While meeting such people as Charlotte Mason, Alain Locke, Zora Neale Hurston, and Wallace Thurman, Hughes had been a man filled with childlike hope and wonder. Now, after weathering some troubled times, he knew that his days of innocence were over.

7

Radical Times

When Hughes returned to New York from Haiti, in August 1931, the Great Depression was almost two years old and the economy showed no signs of recovery. "Had I started looking for work, a job would have been hard to find. Thousands were out of work," he said. "But I did not want a job. I wanted to continue to be a poet."

Freed from the constraints of his relationship with Charlotte Mason, Hughes became much more politically radical than he had been before. Deeply interested in how the depression was affecting America's middle and lower classes, he formed a close association with the John Reed Club, a group made up mostly of writers and intellectuals who shared his left-wing views of social and political issues. He also began writing for the magazine *New Masses* and became a director of a traveling repertory company called the New York Suitcase Theater. The John Reed Club, the Suitcase Theater, and *New Masses* all had close connections with America's Communist party. Hughes always denied being a member of the party, even though he admired many of the positions the party took on various disputes.

One action taken by the Communist party that earned Hughes's respect was its quick and vigorous defense of nine black youths convicted in the Scottsboro case. Just when Hughes was leaving for Cuba and Haiti in March 1931, the youths had been arrested and nearly lynched in Alabama for allegedly raping two white women. All of the people involved in the case—the alleged victims as well as the alleged assailants—had been riding illegally on a train, where the crimes were said to have taken place. Although the evidence against the accused young men was weak, an all-white jury found all nine to be guilty. One of them received a sentence of life imprisonment; the other eight were given the death penalty. Many American citizens were shocked by the proceedings of the trial and considered it a miscarriage of justice. Yet most black organizations, including the NAACP, felt that they had to be careful when it came to aiding the convicted youths. The one group that became outspoken in its efforts to defend the youths was the Communist party.

Hughes was given an excellent opportunity to express his political views when he was told that he would be granted a fellowship of $1,000 from the Julius Rosenwald Fund simply if he applied for it. Hughes drafted a proposal, outlining his plan for a poetry-reading tour through the South "to create an interest in racial expression through books and to do what I can to encourage young black literary talent among our people." His proposal was approved, and he used part of the grant to purchase a car to take him from place to place. He used another part of the grant to establish a small publishing company called Golden Stair Press. (For additional information on Julius Rosenwald and his philanthropy, enter "Julius Rosenwald" into any search engine and browse the sites listed.)

Hughes was drawn to the Communist Party when he heard of its defense of the Scottsboro boys, nine youths convicted of rape in Alabama on minimal evidence. Though he never became a member of the party, Hughes shared many of its beliefs and its willingness to vigorously defend its stances.

Hughes's aim was to publish inexpensive, attractive paperback editions of his poems to be sold to his audiences in the South. Called *The Negro Mother and Other Dramatic Recitations*, these volumes of verse did not contain the fiery and radical poems Hughes was sending to *New Masses*. *The Negro Mother* contained softer poems that would not offend a conservative and religious black audience. Hughes knew that he could not overwhelm his Southern audience with fury; rather, he had to seduce them with sentiment and charm. He also commissioned his New York publisher to print a cheaper, one-dollar edition of his earlier collection, *The Weary Blues*, which he took with him to the South.

Hughes left for his tour on November 2, 1931, from the 135th Street YMCA in Harlem—the same place he had stayed 10 years earlier, when he first came to New York. His car was filled with books and posters advertising the tour and was driven by Radcliffe Lucas, a friend from Lincoln University. Their first stop, at a black trade school in Philadelphia, was followed by stops at several black colleges in Virginia.

In undertaking this journey, Hughes was not indulging in a pleasure trip but embarking on a literary and political campaign "by taking poetry, *my* poetry, to *my* people." His purpose put him in danger of physical violence, for the South in the early 1930s was a particularly dangerous place for blacks.

During the first weekend of Hughes's tour, two unfortunate racial incidents occurred in the South. In one of the incidents, the football coach of Alabama A&M Institute in Normal, Alabama, was beaten to death after mistakenly parking his car in a "white" parking lot while attending a football game. In the other incident, Julia Derricotte, dean of women at Fisk University in Nashville, Tennessee, died after she was refused admission to a whites-only hospital following a car accident.

MILITANT POETRY

One of the more controversial stops on Hughes's tour was made at the University of North Carolina at Chapel Hill. Hughes was invited to lecture there by two students who were members of the local chapter of the John Reed Club. These students published a leftist campus newspaper called *Contempo*, and they released an issue of the newspaper, featuring a militant poem that Hughes had sent them, to coincide with his arrival on campus. The poem, entitled "Christ in Alabama," contains provocative language and a harsh commentary on Southern justice and race relations. The publication of the poem, which concludes with the lines "Nigger Christ / On the cross of the South," touched off a furor not only in Chapel Hill but throughout the South.

Hughes had to receive police protection while he held a reading at the University of North Carolina.

The commotion at Chapel Hill gave Hughes's tour a publicity boost, yet the tour had been well received even before Hughes reached North Carolina. His stock of *The Negro Mother* sold out only a week after he left New York, and more copies had to be shipped to him. Proceeding through South Carolina, Georgia, and Florida, Hughes usually ended his readings with "I, Too, Sing America," the poem he had written while he was stranded in Genoa, Italy.

Hughes pushed the tour at an exhausting pace through Alabama, where he visited the young men convicted in the Scottsboro case in their prison cells on death row. He then went on to Tennessee, Missouri, Kansas, and Oklahoma. After taking a short break to return to New York in March 1932, he resumed the tour in Texas and continued on to New Mexico, Arizona, and California. He ended the tour in San Francisco, where he rested as a guest in the home of a wealthy admirer, Noel Sullivan.

While Hughes was in California, he received a telegram from his friend and former typist, Louise Thompson. The two had discussed work on a movie about American blacks while he had been in New York back in March. The movie was to be filmed in the Soviet Union and financed by the Soviet film company Meschrabpom. The making of the film had been approved by the Soviet government. Thompson's telegram read that the participants in the project—including Hughes, who was to work on the script—were to assemble in New York and then sail to Russia in June. "This unexpected chance to work in films in Russia seemed to open a new door to me," Hughes said. "At that time Hollywood did not employ Negro writers."

Hughes and a group of 21 other members of the film project arrived in Leningrad on June 25, 1932. They checked into the Hotel Metropole in Moscow 10 days later and began work on the film, called *Black and White*, two months after that. Directed by an inexperienced German filmmaker, the film had a script that appeared to Hughes to have been written in Russian by a committee of bureaucrats who had no knowledge of how people really lived in the United States. When a poorly translated version of the script reached Hughes, he was astonished to find that the plot outline called for black steelworkers in the South to appeal to their rich black friend in Birmingham, Alabama, to send a message for help against racism on their private radio station. This appeal for help was directed to the white steelworker comrades in the North. A typical scene in the script depicted the son of a wealthy white Southern industrialist dancing at a party in his father's house with a young black maid.

The project had other problems besides the poor screenplay. Most of the group of actors from New York were amateurs who were unfamiliar with Southern blues and work songs. No sets had been built. No costumes had been made. No

IN HIS OWN WORDS...

In 1935, the influence of what he had seen and experienced in Russia was clear in Hughes's essay "To Negro Writers," which was published in *American Writer's Congress*, edited by Henry Hart. The essay expresses Hughes's beliefs that the principles of socialism and civil rights contained common ground and that the struggle for equal rights was, in many ways, a class struggle as well:

> We want a new and better America, where there won't be any poor, where there won't be any more Jim Crow, where there won't be any lynchings, where there won't be any munition makers, where we won't need philanthropy, nor charity, nor the New Deal, nor Home Relief.
> We want an America that will be ours, a world that will be ours—we Negro workers and white workers! Black writers and white!
> We'll make that world!

contract between the company and any members of Hughes's group had been signed. By August, when shooting should have been well under way, the project collapsed in disarray and confusion.

As compensation for the failed project, the American group was offered a chance by the Russian film company to go on a tour of the country in September. Hughes toured central Asia, intending to write a series of articles for the Soviet newspaper *Izvestia* on the treatment of ethnic minorities in the Soviet Union. On the steppes of Turkistan, Hughes met Arthur Koestler, a journalist who was to become famous for his myth-shattering book about communism, *Darkness at Noon*. The two reporters traveled together for some time, sharing their observations of Russian society.

Hughes had arrived in the Soviet Union feeling sympathy for the people and their leadership, who were trying to solve many political and social problems. Like many artists and intellectuals of the 1930s, he saw the Soviet system as a symbol of hope and as a model for action. Even though the communist government had then been in power for only 15 years and the country was still undeniably poor, he felt that much progress in their society had been made. For one thing, Hughes did not see any obvious signs of racism. Class and racial barriers were being attacked, literacy programs were being initiated, and free medical clinics were being established for all. These were far greater improvements than those Hughes saw taking place in his own country, where a record number of people were without jobs and were close to starvation. Everyone he saw in the Soviet Union seemed to be working, and he was impressed. What he did not see, or refused to see, were other problems created by the Soviet system: the labor camps, the arrest of anyone who disagreed with the state, or the corruption of party officials.

Hughes's tour of Russia lasted until January, when the group returned to Moscow. Most of the remaining members

The Kremlin in Moscow, Russia, houses the offices of Russian government and is the center of Russian political life. During his travels around Russia in 1933, Hughes was impressed by the Russian political system, which he viewed as attacking racism and classism while providing for the underprivileged.

of the film project then returned to the United States. With the depression there growing worse, Hughes decided to remain abroad, writing bold poetry and more conventional short stories. Some of the poems were eventually published in *New Masses*, but when Hughes later tried to publish a collection of them in a book entitled *Good Morning, Revolution*, he was unsuccessful. Even his friend and chief publishing ally, Carl Van Vechten, thought the work too radical to gain much acceptance in the United States.

During Hughes's last few months in Russia, he was re-introduced to Sylvia Chen, a Moscow-based dancer of Chinese ancestry whom he had met the previous fall in Harlem. Before long, the two of them began to talk about getting married. The marriage never took place, but Hughes felt so strongly about her that marriage was a subject he continued to discuss in letters with her even after he returned to the United States.

Hughes finally left Russia in June 1933, traveling on the Trans-Siberian railroad to Vladivostok. From there he journeyed to Japan, took a side trip to Shanghai in China (where he was invited to dinner with Madame Sun Yat-sen, the widow of the great Chinese statesman), and finally sailed across the Pacific for the United States. He landed in San Francisco in early August.

Within a year's time, Hughes had traveled completely around the world.

8

Travels and Travails

While Hughes was in Russia, he had developed the idea of writing a series of short stories whose most important theme would be the relationship between blacks and whites. He had returned to the United States with almost no money, however, so finding the time to work on the project seemed to be a concern. He had to figure out a way of making a living.

Hughes's friend Noel Sullivan solved this problem in one stroke. He offered the 31-year-old poet the use of his second house, called Ennesfree, which was located in the quaint seaside hamlet of Carmel-by-the-Sea, several hours south of San Francisco. Hughes accepted this offer at once. He liked Sullivan and sensed that as a patron Sullivan, unlike Charlotte Mason, would leave him alone with his work.

Ennesfree was a light and airy, two-bedroom cottage with a view of the Pacific Ocean. Hughes was allowed to live there rent free, with Sullivan providing for his food and a cook. The village of Carmel, which then consisted of around a thousand people, had been conceived as an artists' colony in the late nineteenth century. By 1933 a number of painters, writers, and photographers still lived there, but it had also become a retirement community for the wealthy.

Hughes was welcomed as an honored guest by the artists who lived in Carmel, among them the former muckraking journalist Lincoln Steffens, the photographer Edward Weston, and the sculptor Jo Davidson. Most of the Carmel artists belonged to the local chapter of the John Reed Club, and Hughes joined them. He also started to work on some short stories. Many of these touched on the relationships between blacks and whites. Hughes's literary agent, Max Lieber, worked hard to place these stories in major magazines, but he met with only limited success. Lieber was told that the stories were too shocking. Americans in the midst of the depression wanted to read about subjects that would make them forget their problems rather than dwell on subjects that would not go away. (For additional information on John Reed and John Reed Clubs, enter "John Reed" into any search engine and browse the sites listed.)

Despite being unable to find an audience for Hughes's work, Lieber encouraged him to continue with his writing. By December 1933, Hughes had written enough of these stories for a book-length collection. He sent them to Carl Van Vechten in New York, who liked them and helped to get them published in 1934 under the title *The Ways of White Folks.*

The gritty, ironic stories collected in *The Ways of White Folks* were well received, although a few critics bristled over Hughes's representation of patronizing white liberals. The acclaim for *The Ways of White Folks* cheered Hughes. He said that this was "the first long period in my life when I was able, unworried and unhurried, to stay quietly in one place and devote myself to writing," and it proved that with such devotion he could be successful.

Left-wing radical journalist John Reed in an early twentieth-century portrait. Reed's writings exposing social and political issues around the world helped him acquire a following among his fellow writers and intellectuals.

Through the Carmel John Reed Club, Hughes became active in 1934 in farmworkers' strikes and in a longshoremen's strike. The longshoremen's strike in San Francisco was a particularly bloody and disruptive affair. The California media soon began accusing the strikers and their supporters of being Communists whose real goal was to overthrow the government. The local Carmel newspaper subsequently began putting pressure on the John Reed Club. Calls for the police to hold and question club members began to appear in print, and in July 1934 an American Legion post was formed to counter what was perceived as the "menace" of the John Reed Club. Hughes, the only black member of the Carmel branch, was singled out for attack, with one newspaper calling him "a tireless advocate for Soviet Rule, for Communism in this country." With the situation in Carmel becoming increasingly hostile, Hughes decided to leave Ennesfree for the relative safety of San Francisco.

Throughout this period of controversy, Hughes kept to his work schedule. He collaborated with Lincoln Steffens's wife, Ella Winter, on a play called *Blood on the Fields*, based on the agricultural strikes in California. He worked on the memoirs of his journey to the Soviet Union, which he titled *From Harlem to Samarkand*. He wrote a few poems in the ultramilitant style he had developed when he was in the Soviet Union, including "One More 'S' in the U.S.A.," a verse read to the eighth convention of the U.S. Communist Party in 1934:

> Put one more *S* in the U.S.A.
> To make it Soviet.
> One more *S* in the U.S.A.
> Oh, we'll live to see it yet.
> When the land belongs to the farmers
> And the factories to the working men
> The U.S.A. when we take control
> Will be the U.S.S.A. then . . .

Before long, he was asked to head the Communist party's major black organization, the League of Struggle for Negro Rights.

Despite Hughes's productivity, he was having some trouble with his career as a writer. Even with its excellent reviews, *The Ways of White Folks* did not sell well. Max Lieber had a hard time placing Hughes's stories in magazines. Knopf, his New York publisher, rejected *From Harlem to Samarkand*. *Blood on the Fields* was turned down by the Theater Union of New York, a group Hughes had hoped would produce the play.

A TIME OF CHANGE

Feeling that he had reached yet another low point in his life, Hughes decided that it was once again time to move on. He left California for Reno, Nevada, where he found a cheap room in Reno's small black ghetto. With his bank account overdrawn and his writing failing to find an audience, he informed Lieber about a scheme he was attempting out of desperation: he had begun writing sentimental short stories that featured only conventional white characters. Writing under the pseudonym of David Boatman, Hughes would try to pass himself off as a white author. He never got the chance to carry out this scheme completely, however. Several weeks after he started writing stories as David Boatman, he learned that his father had died in Mexico.

Borrowing $150 from his New York publisher and cashing a check from *Esquire* magazine for one of the few stories he had managed to have published, Hughes headed south in December 1934 to pay his last respects to his father and settle the estate he had left. Hughes had not seen his father since 1921, and they had exchanged few letters in the intervening years. Yet James Hughes had always managed to have a powerful hold on his son's psyche, and his death gave Langston a sense of release.

Hughes stayed in Mexico City with his father's longtime friends, the three Patiño sisters, who had been willed James Hughes's entire estate. The sisters insisted that Hughes take a quarter of the estate for himself. After initially resisting their offer, he accepted a portion of the small amount of cash left in his father's bank account.

Jose Antonio Fernández de Castro, Hughes's friend from Cuba who had become a translator of Hughes's work, was

In the mid-1930s, Hughes' productivity soared but his writing career stalled. Though his material was well reviewed, he had trouble finding an audience and his works were continually rejected by magazines, publishers, and producers.

living in Mexico City at that time as a consular officer at the Cuban embassy. Hughes reestablished his friendship with Fernández de Castro as well as with Miguel Covarrubias, the illustrator of Hughes's first book *The Weary Blues*, soon after his 33rd birthday. Within weeks of their reunion, Hughes slipped comfortably into the bohemian life of Mexico City. In March he left the Patiño sisters' house to share an apartment with a new friend, the young French photographer Henri Cartier-Bresson.

Hughes stayed in Mexico City until June, leading the life of a famous expatriate while coming to grips with the sense of freedom he felt after his father's death. He then left Mexico to visit his mother, who was living in Oberlin, Ohio. On his way to visit her, he stopped off in Los Angeles, where he stayed with an old friend from New York, Arna Bontemps. Hughes decided to spend the summer collaborating with Bontemps on a children's book, *Paste Board Bandits*, based on tales Hughes had heard over the years in Mexico. Despite his friend Wallace Thurman's unsuccessful experience in Hollywood, Hughes also tried to break into the lucrative screenwriting trade. Like Thurman, he had little success. Hollywood was not in the habit of employing black writers.

While Hughes was in Mexico, he was chosen to receive a Guggenheim Foundation grant. The Guggenheim fellowship is one of the most prestigious grants given to American artists and writers. The choice of Hughes as a recipient showed that, despite his recent problems in publishing his work, his reputation as a writer was still intact. He was to receive a $1500 grant to work on a novel about urban black life.

WRITING FOR THE THEATER

Hughes labored fitfully for a year on the novel, but he felt that his inspiration for this work was missing. Instead, he turned his attention to the theatre.

Mulatto, a play he had written in 1930, resurfaced thanks to John Rumsey, Hughes's theatrical agent. Rumsey had found a wealthy, young producer-director named Martin Jones who wanted to produce *Mulatto* on Broadway in New York. Hughes agreed to let Jones develop *Mulatto*, but he soon lost control of his work. Instead of developing Hughes's play as a serious exploration about a mulatto (a person with mixed black and white ancestry), Jones sensationalized the play. He created a piece of commercial theater featuring much sex but little in the way of coherent plot or character development. *Mulatto* opened in October 1935 to good notices for the actors but dreadful reviews for Hughes, including one from the New York *World-Telegram*, calling *Mulatto* "not a play [but] an attempt to dramatize an inferiority complex." Most reviewers seemed unaware that Jones had virtually rewritten the play.

Hughes had more success on a smaller scale with two plays produced by the Gilpin Players in Cleveland in 1936. One of the plays, *Troubled Island*, was the revision of the singing play Hughes began on his trip to Cuba in 1930. The other, *Joy to My Soul*, was a farce he wrote in 1936 while he was working in Cleveland with the Gilpin Players. Perhaps as a result of Martin Jones's instincts for commercialization, *Mulatto* became a hit,

A Critical Look at Hughes

In 1934, Langston Hughes published a series of short stories that focused on the relationship between blacks and whites; it was called *The Ways of White Folks*. The stories received mixed reviews; some were praiseworthy, but others took offense with Hughes's depiction of the races.

On July 1, 1934, the *New York Times* offered praise for Hughes' willingness to challenge those who wished to paint a rosy picture of America's race relations in its review of his book, written by Leane Zugsmith:

> Mr. Hughes is a talented writer; he is also a Negro; and it is difficult to decide which comes first. As an artist, it may be a limitation that he concerns himself entirely with the interrelations of the black and white peoples. It was undoubtedly his intention to include only such stories in this collection, and he is not limited in his perceptions and knowledge of either Negroes or whites.
>
> He writes about the impact of one race upon the other with the confidence of the intelligent, self-respecting man. He is scornful of the meretricious friendliness that certain pretentious whites offer to Negroes. He deplores the slave-conditioned, scraping humility that certain Negroes possess. He can be amused as well as infuriated, malicious as well as tender. Perhaps it is because he is none of these things to excess that what he has to say is so effective. . . .

and by 1937 Hughes began receiving fairly large royalty checks. Although these royalties may have provided him with some consolation, Hughes still foundered in his art. He wrote few poems of note, and though he occasionally sold a few stories, the income he earned from these stories was not enough to let him support himself. Once again, he felt a trip was necessary for him to reestablish his work.

In July 1937 Hughes returned to Paris for the first time since his days at the Grand Duc. Europe in 1937 was a much more somber place than it had been in 1924. Spain was entering the second year of a civil war, and events elsewhere in Europe seemed to indicate that a full-scale war was close at hand for the rest of the continent.

In Paris, the music still blew all night at the jazz clubs, and Hughes's friend Bricktop had become a big star. Yet the frantic nightlife betrayed a sense of desperation, not joy. Like the United States, Europe had been ravaged by economic depression.

While Hughes was in Paris, he spent several weeks as a delegate to the International Writers' Congress. Invited to the congress by the French writer André Malraux, among others, Hughes joined his fellow writers at the congress in a protest of fascist attempts to overthrow the Republican government in the civil war in Spain. During one of the meetings of the congress, Hughes told the audience, "In America, Negroes do not have to be told what fascism is in action. We know. Its theories of Nordic supremacy and economic suppression have long been realities to us."

Among the writers attending the congress were Nicolás Guillén and Jacques Roumain. Both men had become Communists since Hughes had last seen them, and both had served time in prison in their respective countries. After the conference ended, Hughes and Guillén, who had become a journalist, traveled to Spain to help the Republicans in their civil war. Hughes worked there as a reporter for the Associated Press and the Baltimore *Afro-American* for six months. He made a number of visits to the battlefront and interviewed black members of the Lincoln Brigade, the American volunteer force siding with the Republican army. He also worked as a reporter and press aide for the Alianza di Intelectuales Antifascistas (Alliance of Antifascist Intellectuals), a public relations and propaganda bureau made up of writers and artists. Through the Alianza he met several notable Americans who were helping the Republican cause, including Ernest Hemingway, Lillian Hellman, and Dorothy Parker. He also reencountered Louise Thompson.

The tragic suffering of the Spanish people during this bloody civil war sparked Hughes's creative imagination in such poems as "Madrid, 1937." These poems, although political,

IN HIS OWN WORDS...

Hughes was impressed by the Lincoln Brigade's efforts during the Spanish Civil War. In *The Volunteer for Liberty*, published in 1937, he wrote of the heroism of these men and others he encountered, setting them in the global context of the civil rights movement, as in this excerpt from "Negroes in Spain":

And now, in Madrid, Spain's besieged capital, I've met wide-awake Negroes from various parts of the world—New York, our Middle West, the French West Indies, Cuba, Africa—some stationed here, others on leave from their battalions—all of them here because they know that if Fascism creeps across Spain, across Europe, and then across the world, there will be no more place for intelligent young Negroes at all. In fact, no decent place for any Negroes—because Fascism preaches the creed of Nordic supremacy and a world for whites alone.

In Spain, there is no color prejudice. Here in Madrid, heroic and bravest of cities, Madrid where the shells of Franco plow through the roof-tops at night, Madrid where you can take a street car to the trenches, this Madrid whose defense lovers of freedom and democracy all over the world have sent food and money and men—here to this Madrid have come Negroes from all the world to offer their help.

Members of the Lincoln Brigade, the American volunteer force which helped defend the Republican army against fascist attacks in the Spanish Civil War. Throughout 1937, Hughes lived in Spain covering the war as a reporter.

were not as radical as the ones he had written after visiting Russia only four years before. The pressure of having to live off his literary wits had mellowed him somewhat. Hughes had begun to realize that there was little point in fighting the conservative forces in America as relentlessly as he had been doing. If he was to live and work, some adjustment in his approach to writing had to be made.

9

The Wandering Poet

After visiting the battlefields of Spain, Hughes decided to write real-life dramas "that will be equal to anybody's battlefront." He returned to New York in early 1938 and began to write and produce plays for the Harlem Suitcase Theater, which he co-founded with Louise Thompson. Borrowing some of the revolutionary techniques he had seen in Russian theater, Hughes wrote and then directed the most remarkable theatrical work of his career, *Don't You Want to Be Free?* Performed on a bare stage, the play is a montage of sermons, dramatic vignettes, poetry, exhortations, and blues songs. *Don't You Want to Be Free?* captured the imagination of its audience and played to capacity crowds until the end of the Suitcase Theater's first season.

In 1939, Hughes returned to Los Angeles. Arna Bontemps had interested the black film actor and musician Clarence Muse in adapting one of Bontemps's novels, *God Sends*

Sunday, into a film script. Hughes was asked to join the project as a scriptwriter. The film, which was retitled *Way Down South*, was also reworked by its producer, Sol Lesser. Hughes found working in Hollywood to be a humiliating experience. "Hollywood," he said, "has spread in exaggerated form every ugly and ridiculous stereotype of the deep South's conception of Negro characters." While he was there he earned more money on a consistent basis than he had ever before, but his employment as a scriptwriter did not last for long. Once *Way Down South* was completed, Hughes was not offered any more film work.

Hughes spent the early part of 1940 working on his autobiography, *The Big Sea*, which tells in brilliantly clear language the story of his life up to the year 1931. One of his most successful efforts at prose writing, *The Big Sea* won generally favorable reviews, although its sales were disappointingly small.

After writing plays, film scripts, and prose, Hughes returned to writing poetry and going on reading tours. In 1942 he returned to Harlem, splitting the rent on an apartment with his childhood friends Emerson and Toy Harper. He maintained a share of an apartment in Harlem for the rest of his life.

Although Hughes had clearly tempered his left-wing radicalism by the early 1940s, he remained as committed as ever to his ideals of social justice and racial equality. Consequently, he eagerly helped with the American war effort when the United States entered World War II in December 1941. He joined the Writers War Board, penning articles for army newspapers, composing lyrics with W.C. Handy and Clarence Muse for war blues to be sung at rallies, and thinking up jingles to spur on the troops along with jingles to combat segregation, such as "Look like by now / Folks ought to know / It's hard to beat Hitler / Protecting Jim Crow."

Hughes's contribution to American literature began to be recognized by more and more people after the war was over. He was appointed poet-in-residence at Atlanta University in

---

HARLEM SUITCASE THEATRE OPENS ITS SECOND SEASON

(Sponsored By Lodge 691, International Workers Order)

SUNDAY, OCTOBER 30th, 9 P. M.

I.W.O. COMMUNITY CENTER, 317 WEST 125th STREET

●

HILARIOUS HISTRIONICS IN FIVE SCENES

FROM UNCLE TOM'S CABIN TO		
EM-FUEHRER JONES	**S**	"One Pancake To Another"
OR		
THE TABLES TURNED		"I Am The Law—For Three"
INCLUDING	**E**	"Joe Kayoe Hitler"
LIMITATIONS OF LIFE		
And		
JERSEY CITY JUSTICE		Above All
AS PRESENTED BY THE ART AND ARTISTS OF	**E**	"Little Eva's End"
THE HARLEM SUITCASE THEATRE		

A Series of Pre-views of skits for a Revue Written by the Theatre Staff

AND

DON'T YOU WANT TO BE FREE?

A POETIC DRAMA BY LANGSTON HUGHES AND DIRECTED BY HILARY PHILLIPS

Regular Performances of this Double Bill Every Sunday Throughout November

Maintaining Our Popular Admission Price of 35c

●

Forthcoming Productions:

YOUNG MAN OF HARLEM, by Powell Lindsay

FUENTE OVEJUNA Adapted by Dorothy Peterson and Langston Hughes from the Spanish of Lope de Vega

FRONT PORCH, by Langston Hughes

ORGANIZER, A folk opera   Libretto by Langston Hughes. Music by James P. Johnson.

Special Prices for Theatre Parties and Benefits—For information Call Algonquin 4-2321.

After returning from Spain, Hughes had great success working with the Harlem Suitcase Theater, which he co-founded with Louise Thompson. His most acclaimed play, *Don't You Want to Be Free?*, a real-life drama which used techniques from Russian theater, sold out the Harlem Suitcase Theater throughout its first season.

1947 and held a position as poet-teacher at the University of Chicago in 1949. He also translated into English works written by his friends, including Jacques Roumain and Nicolás Guillén, among others. His opera libretto, *Troubled Island,* was performed by the New York City Opera Company on March 31, 1949. Leopold Stokowski called it "one of the most inspired expressions of Negro art in the United States."

Among Hughes's most important works of this time was a long-term project that he began in 1943. He created a character named Jesse B. Semple and made him the focus of dozens of short stories. These stories were written originally as part of a regular column for *The Chicago Defender,* a weekly black newspaper, before appearing regularly in the *New York Post.* Collected in four books, the stories chronicled the highs and lows, the frustrations and triumphs, of an Afro-American Everyman, Jesse Semple (also known as Simple). The stories capture the essence of Hughes's personality: his wit, his humor, and his generosity of spirit. "The character of My Simple-Minded Friend is really very simple," he said. "It is just myself talking to me."

Jesse Semple does not seem to be a fighter. He does not directly challenge racist obstacles, but he does confront the problems of everyday life with humor and quiet determination. During Hughes's lifetime, the Semple stories became his most popular work among blacks, and he wrote them for 23 years.

A VIEW OF HARLEM

Hughes's most ambitious poetry collection, *Montage of a Dream Deferred,* was published in 1951. As the title indicates, this volume of poems makes use of the startling montage technique Hughes first incorporated in his play *Don't You Want to Be Free?* It presents a series of images from everyday life in Harlem as seen by the poet. Although the poems may seem to have been arranged at random, Hughes meant the collection to be viewed as a united narrative. The montage of poems takes the reader through one complete day and night in Harlem.

In some of these poems, Hughes uses a writing style to mirror bebop, the new jazz style that had just appeared in

Harlem. No matter what the writing style of the poems are in
Montage of a Dream Deferred, Hughes tackles the problem of
being black in America. In "Harlem," the most famous poem
in the collection, he asks:

> What happens to a dream deferred?
> Does it dry up
> like a raisin in the sun?
>
> Or fester like a sore—
> And then run?
> Does it stink like rotten meat?
> Or crust and sugar over—
> Like syrupy sweet?
>
> Maybe it just sags
> like a heavy load.
>
> Or does it explode?

During the time he was preparing *Montage of a Dream
Deferred* for publication, Hughes's name began to appear in
testimonies being given before congressional committees
investigating the influence of communism in the United
States. These investigations occurred during a time when
anti-Communist feelings in the United States had turned into
a nationwide hysteria. Many loyal citizens found their reputations sullied by false accusations or misleading statements
that they were Communists. Such accusations were presented
before both the Senate committee headed by Joseph McCarthy,
a senator from Wisconsin, and the House Un-American
Activities Committee. On March 26, 1953, Hughes was finally
called to come before the McCarthy committee. His pro-
Communist sympathies were well known and documented in
his writings. In a deal arranged before he gave his testimony,

Langston Hughes speaking before the House Un-American Activities Committee in 1953. Because of his sometimes radical writings and his sympathy for Communism and the Soviet government, Hughes was called to testify before the Committee but was not jailed or forced to name names. However, he did suffer from a loss of revenue due to cancellations and protests on his reading tour.

Hughes agreed to cooperate with the committee by admitting his past radicalism and his prior association with groups allied with the Communist party. In exchange for this admission, he did not have to name specific persons as collaborators. This arrangement was a relatively lenient one for Hughes. Many witnesses before the committee were either jailed when they refused to testify or were coerced into publicly accusing their former friends and colleagues. Other people called to come before the committee, such as Hughes's literary agent, Max Lieber, fled the country in order to avoid giving testimony.

Although no charges of any kind were ever filed against Hughes, and although he had committed no crime—unless speaking one's conscience is considered a crime—his overall character was called into question by the committee. A number of groups canceled Hughes's appearances on his reading tours, and some of his readings were picketed. For a while, these cancellations affected Hughes's ability to earn a living.

FINAL YEARS

Nonetheless, Hughes persevered. He collaborated with photographer Roy de Carava in *Sweet Flypaper of Life* (1955) and with Milton Meltzer in *A Pictorial History of the Negro People in America* (1955), doing research and writing for both projects. *I Wonder As I Wander,* the second of his autobiographies, was published during this time. In this volume Hughes wrote about the people and events of his life up until 1938. In 1959 a retrospective of 40 years of his poetry was published in *Selected Poems.* Although the poems in this collection, all chosen by Hughes, include most of the major poems of his career, it is significant to note some of the poems that Hughes chose to leave out. None of his militant verses from the 1930s are included, nor are many of his scathing poems mocking religion and American justice. In seeking to gain respectability, Hughes stopped being so politically—but not racially— militant. By omitting some important poems, such as "Advertisement for the Waldorf-Astoria" and "Christ in Alabama," he in effect rewrote his personal and professional history for a generation of readers.

In the last decade of Hughes's life, he devoted much of his energy to reviewing the fiction of young black writers, including the novelist James Baldwin and the poet Gwendolyn Brooks. Hughes also became involved with the government as a spokesman for American culture. Such involvement was made possible by the relatively liberal administrations of Presidents John F. Kennedy and Lyndon Johnson in the 1960s.

He visited Europe and Africa several times as an official cultural emissary of the U.S. State Department.

Hughes also continued to write plays in the 1960s, but these productions met with little commercial success. In two of them, *Gospel Glow* and *Tambourines to Glory*, Hughes attempted to bring to the stage dramatic interpretations of black religion as experienced through gospel music. He believed that gospel music was an important folk tradition in Afro-American culture, and he thought its intense emotional experience could be successfully transformed into powerful theater. In spite of some favorable reviews, these two plays had short runs in New York's off-Broadway theaters in 1962 and 1963, respectively.

Hughes's health began to fail in the spring of 1967. When he experienced a physical attack so severe that it made him fear for his life, he checked into a public hospital under his given name, James Hughes, where he was diagnosed with prostate cancer. He remained in the hospital for three weeks. After an operation on his prostate gland on May 19, his condition worsened, and he died on May 22, 1967, at the age of 65. His funeral was held, in accordance with the instructions in his will, in a Harlem funeral home, not in a church. According to his request, a jazz band was hired to celebrate, rather than mourn, his memory.

LEGACY

By the time of his death, Hughes had already been honored by many universities and institutions, including the Library of Congress, as the guiding light of black literature around the world. In Hughes's obituary, published on May 23, 1967, the *New York Times* described Hughes as "the O. Henry of Harlem." Quoting an autobiographical sketch Hughes had prepared for the biographical dictionary *Twentieth Century Authors*, the *Times* noted that Hughes described himself with these words: "I live in Harlem, New York City. I am unmarried.

I like 'Tristan,' goat's milk, short novels, lyric poems, heat, simple folk, boats and bullfights; I dislike 'Aida,' parsnips, long novels, narrative poems, cold, pretentious folk, buses and bridges."

These simple phrases belied the dramatic impression Hughes made on American poetry. Yet it was with simple phrases and stark images that Hughes portrayed a very different America from the one with which many readers were familiar: the America of its black citizens—the struggles and frustrations of everyday black life, the rhythm of black music, the voice of a downtrodden people. Critic Lindsay Patterson noted, "Hughes more than any other black poet or writer, recorded faithfully the nuances of black life and its frustrations."

More than three years after his death, Hughes was still producing work, which included the release of the spoken album *Langston Hughes Reads and Talks About His Poetry*, a recording that prompted critic Clayton Riley to write in the *New York Times*: "To an America that betrayed nearly every promise of hope ever made to its Black inhabitants, Langston Hughes offered continuing declarations of personal resiliency. His poetry celebrated survival and endurance, those central ingredients of our experience; and he couched them in humor and irony, a frequently subtle but abiding passion, and finally, a certain sad awareness regarding the impossibility of being Hughes, the Black man, and Hughes, the American."

Hughes's influence transcended the written word. He spoke for an America that many did not believe existed, but more important, he also argued passionately for an America that he believed could exist—an America in which all were equal, in which all could share in the country's bounty and its successes. He did not hesitate to speak out against injustice, but he was also outspoken in his ideas for how that injustice could best be corrected. He believed that black *was* beautiful, but he was open to the ideas and influences of other cultures and other heritages.

Pulitzer Prize-winning author Alice Walker stands with a display of the Langston Hughes commemorative stamp in Lawrence, Kansas, on January 31, 2002. Decades after his death, Hughes continues to inspire writers like Walker with his commitment to exposing racial and social injustice while exploring the unique intricacies of black life.

Long after his death, Hughes has been remembered and honored. On the 89th anniversary of his birth, in 1991, noted writers including Maya Angelou and Amiri Baraka gathered to honor Hughes when his remains were interred beneath the Schomburg Center for Research in Black Culture in Harlem. There, a specially designed tile floor, labeled "I've Known Rivers," provides a commemorative resting place where visitors can remember Hughes and honor his memory. On the 100th anniversary of his birth, in 2002, *The Crisis*, which had so influenced Hughes during his early years, featured him on its cover in a special commemorative issue exploring his life and legacy.

From Nicolás Guillén and Jacques Roumain to Alice Walker and Imamu Amiri Baraka, Hughes showed black writers the importance of writing about racial freedom. In return, he saw blacks in America fight to improve society and blacks in Africa seek to liberate themselves from European rule. These twin movements toward freedom derived their inspiration in no small part from the efforts of Langston Hughes, who, in the long years since he had crossed the Mississippi bridge at St. Louis, had become the poet laureate of the black world.

1902 Born James Langston Hughes in Joplin, Missouri, on February 1

1916 Moves to Cleveland, Ohio; attends Central High School

1919 Travels to Toluca, Mexico, to visit his father

1920 Graduates from high school; writes "The Negro Speaks of Rivers"; publishes his first poem in *The Brownies' Book*

1921 Arrives in New York City; begins his studies at Columbia University

1922 Leaves Columbia; works as a crewman on the *Oronoke*, anchored at Jones Point, New York

1923 Writes "The Weary Blues"; ships out for Africa on the *West Hesseltine*

1924 Travels to the Netherlands and Paris; writes "I, Too, Sing America"

1925 Moves to Washington, D.C.; works for Dr. Carter Woodson; meets Carl Van Vechten and Vachel Lindsay

1926 *The Weary Blues* is published; enters Lincoln University

1927 *Fine Clothes to the Jew* is published; meets Charlotte Mason; travels to the South on first poetry reading tour

1929 Graduates from Lincoln University

1930 Travels to Cuba; Mason breaks off her patronage relationship with him

1931 Visits Cuba and Haiti; begins reading tour of the United States

1932 Works in the Soviet Union on film project; travels as a reporter for *Izvestia*

1933 Lives and works in Carmel, California

1934 Father dies; Hughes travels to Mexico City

1935 *Mulatto* opens on Broadway

1937 Travels to Paris; covers the Spanish Civil War as a reporter

1938   Mother dies; Hughes founds Harlem Suitcase Theater; writes and directs *Don't You Want to Be Free?*

1939   Works in Los Angeles on *Way Down South*

1943   Begins writing Semple stories for a newspaper column

1951   *Montage of a Dream Deferred* is published

1953   Is subpoenaed to testify before McCarthy committee

1960–1963   Travels to Europe and Africa as cultural emissary for U.S. State Department

1967   Dies in New York City on May 22

Berry, Faith. *Langston Hughes: Before and Beyond Harlem.* Westport, Connecticut: Lawrence Hill & Company, 1983.

Huggins, Nathan. *Voices From the Harlem Renaissance.* New York: Oxford University Press, 1976.

Hughes, Langston. *The Big Sea.* New York: Alfred A. Knopf, 1940.

———. *I Wonder as I Wander.* New York: Rhinehart, 1956.

———. *Selected Poetry of Langston Hughes.* New York: Alfred A. Knopf, 1959.

Rampersad, Arnold. *The Life of Langston Hughes: I, Too, Sing America.* Volume 1. New York: Oxford University Press, 1986.

WEBSITES
Academy of American Poets.
www.poets.org

America's Story from America's Library.
www.americaslibrary.gov

Langston Hughes.
www.Nytimes.com/books/01/04/22/specials/hughes.html

page:

3: © CORBIS

8: Photographs and Prints Division, Schomburg Center for Research in Black Culture, The New York Public Library, Astor, Lenox and Tilden Foundations

13: Associated Press, AP

23: © CORBIS

26: © Bettmann/CORBIS

29: © Romare Bearden Foundation/ Licensed by VAGA, New York, NY/Art Resource

33: Library of Congress Map Division

38: © Bettmann/CORBIS

43: © Bettmann/CORBIS

45: © Hulton|Archive by Getty Images

61: © Hulton|Archive by Getty Images

64: © Earl & Nazima Kowall/ CORBIS

68: Associated Press, AP

73: Library of Congress, LC-DIG-ppmsc-03845

77: © Bettmann/CORBIS

80: © Hulton|Archive by Getty Images

85: Associated Press, AP

88: Photographs and Prints Division, The New York Public Library, Astor, Lenox and Tilden Foundations

91: Associated Press, AP

95: Associated Press, AP/ Orlin Wagner

Cover: © Time Life Pictures/Getty Images

ABOUT THE AUTHOR

Jack Rummel is a freelance writer who has written articles about Latin America and the South and has followed the development of Gulf Coast blues for many years. He lives in Hoboken, New Jersey, and is the author of *Malcolm X* and *Muhammad Ali* in the BLACK AMERICANS OF ACHIEVEMENT series published by Chelsea House.

CONSULTING EDITOR, REVISED EDITION

Heather Lehr Wagner is a writer and editor. She is the author of 30 books exploring social and political issues and focusing on the lives of prominent Americans and has contributed to biographies of *Alex Haley, Jesse Owens*, and *Colin Powell*, in the BLACK AMERICANS OF ACHIEVEMENT Legacy Editions. She earned a BA in political science from Duke University and an MA in government from the College of William and Mary. She lives with her husband and family in Pennsylvania.

CONSULTING EDITOR, FIRST EDITION

Nathan Irvin Huggins was W.E.B. Du Bois Professor of History and Director of the W.E.B. Du Bois Institute for Afro-American Research at Harvard University. He previously taught at Columbia University. Professor Huggins was the author of numerous books, including *Black Odyssey: The Afro-American Ordeal in Slavery, The Harlem Renaissance*, and *Slave and Citizen: The Life of Frederick Douglass*. Nathan I. Huggins died in 1989.